Idealism after Existentialism

A century ago, the dominant philosophical outlook was not some form of materialism or naturalism, but idealism. However, this way of thinking about reality fell out of favour in the Anglo-American analytic tradition as well as the Continental schools of the twentieth century. The aim of this book is to restage and reassess the encounter between idealism and contemporary philosophy. The idealist side will be represented by the great figures of the ninteenth-century post-Kantian tradition in Germany, from Fichte and Schelling to Hegel, followed by the towering Hegelians in Britain led by T. H. Green, F. H. Bradley and Bernard Bosanquet. Their twentieth-century adversaries will be represented by the secular existentialists, especially the famous French trio of Sartre, Beauvoir and Camus, who sought to follow Nietzsche in philosophizing in light of the death of God. And the arena of encounter will be the philosophy of religion—more specifically, questions relating to the nature and existence of God, death and the meaning of life, and the problem of evil. The book argues that the existentialist critique of idealism enables an innovative as well as a more critical and adventurous approach that is sorely needed in philosophy of religion today.

Idealism after Existentialism will be of interest to scholars and advanced students working in the history of nineteenth- and twentieth-century philosophy and philosophy of religion.

N. N. Trakakis is Senior Lecturer in Philosophy at the Australian Catholic University. He is the author of *The God Beyond Belief* (2007) and *The End of Philosophy of Religion* (2008). He is also the editor of *The Problem of Evil: Eight Views in Dialogue* (2018) and coeditor, with Graham Oppy, of the five-volume *History of Western Philosophy of Religion* (2009) and the four-volume *Interreligious Philosophical Dialogues* (2018).

Routledge Focus on Philosophy

Routledge Focus on Philosophy is an exciting and innovative new series, capturing and disseminating some of the best and most exciting new research in philosophy in short book form. Peer reviewed and at a maximum of fifty thousand words shorter than the typical research monograph, *Routledge Focus on Philosophy* titles are available in both ebook and print on demand format. Tackling big topics in a digestible format the series opens up important philosophical research for a wider audience, and as such is invaluable reading for the scholar, researcher and student seeking to keep their finger on the pulse of the discipline. The series also reflects the growing interdisciplinarity within philosophy and will be of interest to those in related disciplines across the humanities and social sciences.

Moral Choices for Our Future Selves
An Empirical Theory of Prudential Perception and a
Moral Theory of Prudence
Eleonora Viganò

Moralistics and Psychomoralistics
A Unified Cognitive Science of Moral Intuition
Graham Wood

Idealism after Existentialism
Encounters in Philosophy of Religion
N. N. Trakakis

For more information about this series, please visit: www.routledge.com/Routledge-Focus-on-Philosophy/book-series/RFP

Idealism after Existentialism
Encounters in Philosophy of Religion

N. N. Trakakis

Routledge
Taylor & Francis Group

NEW YORK AND LONDON

First published 2023
by Routledge
605 Third Avenue, New York, NY 10158

and by Routledge
4 Park Square, Milton Park, Abingdon, Oxon, OX14 4RN

Routledge is an imprint of the Taylor & Francis Group, an informa business

© 2023 N. N. Trakakis

The right of N. N. Trakakis to be identified as author of this work has been asserted in accordance with sections 77 and 78 of the Copyright, Designs and Patents Act 1988.

ISBN: 978-1-032-45770-3 (hbk)
ISBN: 978-1-032-45771-0 (pbk)
ISBN: 978-1-003-37862-4 (ebk)

DOI: 10.4324/9781003378624

Typeset in Times New Roman
by codeMantra

Contents

1 Introduction

At the turn of the twentieth century, the dominant philosophical out-look was not some form of materialism or naturalism, as it presently is, but idealism. The idealist view has a long and interesting history in Western philosophy as well as in Eastern religious thought, and although it has been formulated in a wide range of ways, the basic idea is that 'mind' is the only or the primary reality. In modern Western philosophy, important versions of this view were developed by bishop George Berkeley (1685–1753), who defended a theistic variety of subjective idealism (though he liked to call it 'immaterialism'), famously holding that "to be is to be perceived" (*esse est percipi*); the Enlightenment philosopher, Immanuel Kant (1724–1804), who sought to usher in a Copernican revolution in philosophy through his 'transcendental idealism,' according to which the spatio-temporal features of objects are 'empirically real' but 'transcendentally ideal'; and the great post-Kantian philosopher, G. W. F. Hegel (1770–1831), whose system of 'absolute idealism,' despite accusations of pantheism and atheism from traditional theists, was to deeply influence nineteenth-century British philosophers and theologians who saw in Hegel's work the promise of liberating Christianity from the confines of orthodoxy.

These British idealists—whose members included such towering figures as F. H. Bradley, T. H. Green and Bernard Bosanquet—were soon swept away by a younger generation that had grown impatient with and suspicious of the grand metaphysical claims of their venerable elders. This marked the beginning of analytic philosophy, led by G. E. Moore and Bertrand Russell, and a gradual recovery of what they regarded as (in good English empiricist fashion) "a robust sense of reality." For much of the subsequent century, philosophy in the anglo-American world was pursued in accordance with a (logical-linguistic) analytical approach and physicalist paradigm that typically

DOI: 10.4324/9781003378624-1

assumed, and only rarely sought to substantiate, the falsity of idealism. The influence of this method and paradigm has been so great that even though metaphysics has been in full bloom in analytic philosophy for some time now, idealism has only very recently been making something of a comeback.[1]

Historically, there emerged an alternative to idealism that was also largely overlooked by analytic philosophy. This alternative was existentialism, which originated from the ranks of the idealist movement itself (consider the later Schelling, for example). Commenting, however, on the rise of existentialism in the middle of the last century, John Passmore observed that "professional philosophers, for the most part, dismiss it with a contemptuous shrug."[2] The prejudices of these philosophers aside, it's worth highlighting that existentialism stood in a dialectical relationship with idealism, borrowing and continuing important strands of thought from the German idealists while also seeking to challenge many of their assumptions. If, therefore, we wish to reconsider the merits of idealism, it might be worthwhile to return to existentialism and its reasons for rejecting idealism. This is the strategy adopted in the present study.

The arena selected for the encounter between these two systems of thought is the philosophy of religion, given that religious or religious-type questions and concepts loom large in both systems, and both seek in their very different ways to come to grips with the 'death of God.' The British idealists, in particular, sought to develop a metaphysics that could withstand the Victorian crisis of faith, the "melancholy, long, withdrawing roar" of the "sea of faith," as expressed in Matthew Arnold's "Dover Beach" (1867). Also, existentialism—whether religious (Kierkegaardian) or secular (Nietzschean)—cannot be adequately understood without reference to its critical, if sometimes subterranean, dialogue with religion. As Sartre stated, "Existentialism is nothing else but an attempt to draw the full conclusions from a consistently atheistic position."[3]

The battle between idealism and existentialism begins in Chapter 2 with the 'problem of evil,' the challenge of explaining or justifying the presence of evil in a world created and sustained by a perfectly good God. After sketching the principal figures and themes of modern (nineteenth-century German and British) idealism, I discuss the strategies employed by idealist thinkers to address the problem of evil. I then turn to existentialist responses to the problem, differentiating between religious responses and secular ones, and arguing that only the latter offer a convincing way out of the theodical impasses created by traditional theism.

Chapter 3 turns to a long-forgotten controversy in the annals of British idealism concerning the nature and ultimate reality of 'personality,' both human and divine. In reviving this debate, and recontextualizing it within the broader encounter between idealism and existentialism, the goal is to show how idealism falls short in its conception of 'the value and destiny of the individual' (to borrow the title of one of Bosanquet's books). Finally, Chapter 4 draws out the implications of the foregoing existentialist critique for the practice of philosophy today. One of the metaphilosophical lessons to be taken from this critique consists in the need for a less doctrinaire and more 'aporetic' model of inquiry, so as to awake contemporary philosophy of religion from its dogmatic slumber.

Notes

1 See, for example, Benedikt Göcke, *A Theory of the Absolute* (Basingstoke: Palgrave MacMillan, 2014); Howard Robinson, *From the Knowledge Argument to Mental Substance: Resurrecting the Mind* (Cambridge: Cambridge University Press, 2016); Tyron Goldschmidt and Kenneth L. Pearce (eds), *Idealism: New Essays in Metaphysics* (Oxford: Oxford University Press, 2017); Sebastian Rödl, *Self-Consciousness and Objectivity: An Introduction to Absolute Idealism* (Cambridge, MA: Harvard University Press, 2018).
2 Passmore, *A Hundred Years of Philosophy* (London: Gerald Duckworth and Company, 1957), p.459. As Robert Sinnerbrink and Matheson Russell have remarked, "By the early 1960s the contemptuous shrug had become more a vigorous shove, with the clear marking of a 'gulf' or 'divide' now existing between Continental philosophy (phenomenology and existentialism) and Anglophone philosophy (analytic philosophy)" ("Black Swan: A History of Continental Philosophy in Australia and New Zealand," in Graham Oppy and N. N. Trakakis (eds), *History of Philosophy in Australia and New Zealand*, Dordrecht: Springer, 2014, vol. 2, pp.645–6).
3 Jean-Paul Sartre, *Existentialism and Humanism*, trans. Philip Mairet (London: Methuen & Co., 1948), p.56.

Bibliography

Göcke, B. *A Theory of the Absolute* (Basingstoke: Palgrave MacMillan, 2014). https://doi.org/10.1057/9781137412829_1
Goldschmidt, T. and K. L. Pearce (eds), *Idealism: New Essays in Metaphysics* (Oxford: Oxford University Press, 2017). https://doi.org/10.1093/oso/9780198746973.001.0001
Passmore, J. *A Hundred Years of Philosophy* (London: Gerald Duckworth and Company, 1957).

Robinson, H. *From the Knowledge Argument to Mental Substance: Resurrecting the Mind* (Cambridge: Cambridge University Press, 2016). https://doi.org/10.1017/cbo9781316092873

Rödl, S. *Self-Consciousness and Objectivity: An Introduction to Absolute Idealism* (Cambridge, MA: Harvard University Press, 2018). https://doi.org/10.4159/9780674983267

Sartre, J.-P. *Existentialism and Humanism*, trans. P. Mairet (London: Methuen and Co., 1948).

Sinnerbrink, R. and M. Russell. "Black Swan: A History of Continental Philosophy in Australia and New Zealand," in G. Oppy and N. N. Trakakis (eds), *History of Philosophy in Australia and New Zealand* (Dordrecht: Springer, 2014), vol. 2, pp.637–78. https://doi.org/10.1007/978-94-007-6958-8_24

2 "Urge to unmake / all wrought finalities"

Idealism and the Problem of Evil

2.1

John Hick is perhaps best remembered today for his development and defence of the 'soul-making theodicy,' above all in his 1966 classic *Evil and the God of Love*.[1] Hick's primary postulate was that God's overall purpose, in relation to humankind, was to give human creatures both the potential and the means to transcend their narrow but natural self-centredness and enter into a deeper form of relationship with their neighbours and their God. But such self-transformation would necessitate what John Keats called a 'vale of soul-making,' a particularly risky, if not ruinous, world where "there are obstacles to be overcome, tasks to be performed, goals to be achieved, setbacks to be endured, problems to be solved, dangers to be met."[2] A world, that is, with an abundance of evil and suffering and injustice, and with very little evidence of the presence and providence of God, so as to give the appearance at least of the absence of divinity or any divine plan or intervention. A world, in other words, very much like ours.

But Hick was well aware that even such a grand theodicy as this was not enough. There is no doubt that adversity often builds character; as both psychologists and popular biographies regularly remind us, trauma and tragedy can give birth to transformation, bringing hope and meaning to seemingly pointless suffering. But in just as many circumstances, it seems, the suffering remains unredeemed. Suffering may strengthen, but it can also crush and debilitate, even snuff out entirely. It seems, then, that the soul-making process, if it exists at all, is quite ineffective. To circumvent this problem, Hick speculated that this process does not terminate at death, so that anyone unfit for communion with God by the end of their earthly life continues on the course of moral and spiritual growth until they too attain the ultimate heavenly state of an eternal life of love and fellowship with God. Hick,

DOI: 10.4324/9781003378624-2

therefore, appended to his theodicy an eschatology, and a universalist one at that. Indeed, he came to see that any credible theodicy must follow suit. As he liked to put it: *no theodicy without eschatology.*

2.2

W. V. Quine liked to say that one man's *modus ponens* is another's *modus tollens*. If, for instance, there can be no theodicy without eschatology, then the rejection of eschatology entails the rejection of theodicy. The philosophy of 'absolute idealism' provides a good illustration of Hick's postulate in reverse. In short, the absolute idealists—whether they be German (e.g., Hegel) or British (e.g., Bradley), Hindu (e.g., Advaitan) or Buddhist (e.g., Yogacaran)—contend that the category of the 'self' or the 'individual' has no genuine applicability to human beings, but must be reserved for the Absolute alone. There is, on this view, no possibility of postmortem survival as a finite person, self, or individual. Any eschatology of the sort where the sufferings of a human being can be defeated or somehow redeemed or compensated is ruled out in advance. And, by Hick's reasoning, this means that the project of theodicy is also ruled out: there will inevitably be evils and sufferings, which cannot be satisfactorily 'explained' or 'justified'—they will remain forever as surds in the overall scheme of things.

What response, then, can be made to the problem of evil within the framework of absolute idealism? And how does the idealist response fare in comparison with standard theistic responses, like that advanced by Hick? Is the idealist view in the end just as implausible and incredible "in the presence of the burning children" (to borrow from Rabbi Greenberg)?

2.3

To begin with, a brief recapitulation of absolute idealism will be helpful. The system has of course been expressed in diverse ways over many centuries, in both West and East, but the bare essentials may be captured as follows.

Idealism can be understood as the view that *mind* is the most basic reality, and that the physical world exists only as an appearance to or expression of mind, or is somehow mental in its inner essence. More succinctly, *the physical is derivative from mind.*

For absolute idealists, this ultimate mind-like reality is the 'Absolute,' defined broadly as that which has an unconditioned existence (not conditioned by, or dependent upon, anything else) and is "one and all" (Hölderlin's personal motto), in some sense, both unitary and the whole of things. Here are some illustrations of how this may be fleshed out a bit further.

2.3.1

In his 1893 *magnum opus*, *Appearance and Reality*, F. H. Bradley conceived the Absolute as an all-embracing and harmonious Whole, the totality of all things (without being a mere aggregate of them) that consists in a single, seamless, timeless and inconceivably rich 'experience' that can never be adequately conceptualized. This is a version of *monism* (all is one, or in Bradley's case: a one-in-many)[3] as well as of *idealism* (reality is mental or mind-like), and specifically of *absolute* idealism (given that reality is not construed in terms of the contents of the human mind, as in 'subjective' idealism, but in terms of a non- or supra-personal consciousness). Bradley's teacher at Oxford, T. H. Green, described the Absolute in terms that were more vague and abstract, but just as distinctly idealist. Green's Absolute, called by him the 'Eternal Consciousness,' is the underlying ground of all reality, including finite experiences such as our own, and is constituted by a system of relations that is complete and internally coherent. It is eternal in the sense of being timeless (existing atemporally), and it consists in pure consciousness, somewhat like a vastly expanded human mind but without the restraints and limits imposed by our animal existence. Although eternal, it expresses itself over time through the life of the individual and the community; and although universal and infinite, it is not external to the world but thoroughly immanent in it.

2.3.2

The British idealists were working under the inspiration of the post-Kantian tradition of German idealism, where the overriding goal was to 'complete' Kant's efforts in a 'system,' as Fichte put it—that is to say, to 'systematize' Kant by overcoming the confusions and simplifying the categories of the *Critiques*, particularly the various intolerable dualisms therein, such as the split between nature and freedom, noumena and phenomena, and (above all) intuition and concept.[4] According to Kant's successors, the requisite systematicity and order could only be achieved, ironically enough, by returning to a pre-Critical way of philosophizing—that is, by reinvigorating speculative metaphysics, which they attempted through the development of systems of 'absolute idealism.' Understandably, Kant's reaction to this pretence amongst his friends and followers of 'completing' the Critical Philosophy was to repeat an Italian proverb: "May God protect us from our friends, and we shall watch out for our enemies ourselves!"[5]

His 'friends,' undeterred, advanced some of the most audacious claims ever made to have unveiled the mysteries of the universe. Fichte, motivated by contemporary criticisms of the Critical project, put forward his *Wissenschaftslehre* or 'Theory of Scientific Knowledge,' as a more rigorous and integrated version of transcendental idealism than that offered by Kant. This radically new Kantian dispensed with the 'thing-in-itself,' and sought the unifying ground of reality in the freedom of pure self-consciousness, of the self-positing subject or 'I.' Fichte has therefore been called, and understood himself as, "the first philosopher of radical freedom,"[6] giving birth to an unabashedly subjective form of idealism: no passivity is to be found in subjectivity; there is no outside world or object of experience that is not the product of the self's own free positing activity. For Fichte, however, "the I is not the agent, but the acting itself,"[7] and at bottom it is the acting not so much of the empirical self as of the Absolute Ego, a cosmic self or world-spirit striving to work out its destiny in and through the moral struggles of finite individuals. The Absolute Ego, as Robert Solomon points out, "requires particular egos for its manifestation, but it is not limited to any particular ego or group of egos. It is nothing less than the whole of human consciousness—literally, 'consciousness in general,'" the latter term echoing Kant's description of the transcendental ego.[8]

Schelling's idealism was initially as absolute as Fichte's though not as unwavering in the end, as Schelling became notorious (much like Bertrand Russell) for frequently shifting his philosophical position. Solomon observes that "Schelling was publishing a different system every year in the last decade of the eighteenth century, prompting Hegel to comment that 'he was educating himself in public.'"[9] These shifts in outlook were to propel Schelling from being one of the central figures in the German idealist movement at the end of the century to becoming one of its most vocal critics, especially against Hegel (this probably motivating Kierkegaard to attend Schelling's lectures in Berlin): he came to reject not only Fichte's version of idealism but the idealist tradition as a whole, including his own earlier contributions to this tradition (he came to reject, for example, the typical post-Kantian idealist criterion of truth as residing in conceptual completeness: Schelling, like Kierkegaard, eventually opted for 'actual existence'). Before reaching that point, however, Schelling had constructed yet another extravagant system of absolute idealism, what he called

Identitätphilosophie (Identity Philosophy). The Absolute, on this view, consists in the ultimate identity of nature and 'spirit,' of objective reality and subjective consciousness, which are but two aspects of one and the same originary, unconditioned ground, or absolute 'indifference' (again recalling Russell, this time his neutral monism).

For Hegel, however, Schelling's monistic vision, with its Absolute which dissolves all differentiation, appeared as the "night in which all cows are black." Schelling and Hegel's friendship, dating back to their seminary days in Tübingen, would not survive this remark from Hegel's Preface to the *Phenomenology of Spirit*—the book thus serving as "a document of divorce," in Yirmiyahu Yovel's words.[10] One irreconcilable difference concerned the claim of the Jena Romantics (Fichte and Schelling among them) that the Absolute can be directly intuited or felt, unmediated by conceptual reason. By contrast, in Hegel's monumental (some might say pretentious) system, the Absolute can only be discovered at the end of a *dialectical process* of *Aufheben* ('sublation'), where any immediate or primordial unity is negated and reflectively differentiated before being 'raised up' into a new totality or whole. The name Hegel attaches to this progressive unfolding or 'ascent to the whole' is *'Begriff'*—the first principle in Hegel's system, variously rendered as 'Concept,' 'Reason,' or 'Notion,' which systematically explains all of reality, and indeed is what reality is, the conceptual constitution of the way things are: "What is rational is actual and what is actual is rational."[11] As an idealist, Hegel contends that there is no truth or reality in itself, mind-independently; rather, truth lies always within, not beyond, experience, and experience is always mediated through the 'Concept' or the conceptual structure and activity through which we comprehend and determine reality. This emphasis on activity and movement means that the Absolute as the sum total of reality is to be removed from the category of substance (as in Spinoza) and placed on the plane of process—specifically, a process of self-discovery, culminating in reason's recognition of itself as the whole of reality. The Absolute *qua* subject, that is, as universal Spirit (*Geist*)— which "is simply," Solomon explains, "the world, aware of itself as a self-conscious and comprehensible unity"[12]—is engrossed in history and thus developmental in nature, "never at rest but always engaged in moving forward,"[13] progressing in subject-like fashion by negating, differentiating, and positing itself. The goal of this transformative process is the Spirit's acquisition of self-consciousness—a goal only attained, inevitably, in the writing and reading of the *Phenomenology of the Spirit*. By the same token, Hegel's God *qua* Spirit is in process of realizing itself through time and human events, where this entails a process of becoming actual only by achieving self-consciousness through our consciousness of him: "God is God only in so far as he knows himself: his self-consciousness is, further, a self-consciousness in man and man's knowledge of God, which proceeds to man's self-knowledge in God."[14] This may not necessarily reduce the reality of God or the Absolute to human projection or invention, but it does render it wholly immanent. As Paul Redding points out,

> Hegel's God is clearly an immanent *this*-worldly one, dependent on human recognition… God dwells and is made manifest within recognitive practices such as those of confession and forgiveness… That God's mind is, as it were, distributed across the minds of finite human beings, and is reliant on the acts of those finite beings, does not *disqualify* it from being a mind in its own right, nor does this reduce it to the status of a *mere* fiction.[15]

2.3.3

On this view, shared by German and British idealists at large, mind or consciousness (including the mind or consciousness of God) is 'in,' not 'beyond,' experience: there is not some agent *behind* the experience, which *has* it and in consequence unifies it; rather, mind is the very unity of the experience itself. T. H. Green, for example, rejected the atomism of his British empiricist predecessors, and instead found relations at the heart of everything. (Even for Bradley all our basic categories are in one way or another relational.) This led Green, as it did most absolute idealists, to a *monistic* view of reality where nothing is wholly separate from anything else, and the more you probe into existence the more relations you unearth. Reality is therefore seen holistically as a unified relational matrix: everything is related to everything else. There is no self, however, 'behind' the relations, thus subverting any theodical or eschatological scheme such as Hick's.

2.4

Idealism of the foregoing sort is metaphysics on a grand scale, or better yet *Wissenschaft* or 'science' in its nineteenth-century sense as "the most rigorous, thoughtful, and comprehensive treatment of the whole of human experience."[16] *Wissenschaft*, the 'academic password' of the period, as Solomon calls it, exemplified the very ambitions to systematicity and completion that Kant opposed as pre-Critical or 'dogmatic.' Many today, even many who are otherwise deeply indebted to Hegel and idealist thought, would be sympathetic to Kant, in wishing to distance themselves from claims to absolute knowledge, totality and closure. But Hegel himself had other ideas. While he was finishing the *Phenomenology of Spirit*, in October 1806, Hegel was witnessing the swift invasion and defeat of Jena by Prussian troops led by Napoleon, "that world-soul," as Hegel described him in a letter, "who, concentrated here at a single point, astride a horse, reaches out over the world and masters it." "There were many Germans," Solomon states, "who welcomed the intrusion, despite the dangers. To them, Napoleon was not merely a foreign invader; he was the incarnation of the glorious revolution of France which they had avidly followed as students."[17] As Solomon goes on to say, "The dominant image of the epoch was the birth of a new world, a change in the very *concept* of reality."[18] It was not long, however, before this concept was undone by reality.

This trajectory can be charted in T. S. Eliot, who began as a student at Harvard, reading Indian philosophy and later writing a dissertation on F. H. Bradley at Harvard under the supervision of Josiah Royce (but also working on the dissertation during a fellowship taken at Merton College, Oxford, as a pupil of H. H. Joachim, a disciple of Bradley).[19] By the time the dissertation was completed, in April 1916, Eliot had become sceptical of Bradley's idealism and was growing dissatisfied more generally with philosophical theories and totalizing metaphysical systems. And by the time *The Waste Land* was published, in 1922, the defection from idealism was as complete as Russell's and Moore's earlier deconversion. In breaking away from idealism and ushering in a new way of practising philosophy, Russell and Moore felt "a sense of emancipation"—it was now finally possible to hold "that *everything* is real that common sense, uninfluenced by philosophy or theology, supposes real." "The world," Russell stated, "had been thin and logical," while now it "suddenly became rich and varied and solid."[20] The contrast with Eliot could not be greater: the loss of the idealist vision presaged for him the loss of a stable, secure, traditional and communal way of being, where happiness and fulfilment were grounded in relationality, in the self's role in the social organism. The fracturing of the organic whole, as enacted in the fragmented and polyphonic text of *The Waste Land*, was not a cause for celebration or a source of consolation, but of disenchantment and disillusionment, if not nausea and revulsion. By now, in war-ravaged Europe, the previous sense of coherence and purpose had given way to a desiccated 'wasteland,' decaying and spectral cities inhabited by solitary, hollowed and depthless individuals unable to connect or to fathom any final or fundamental justifications. There were many reasons behind this change of perspective, but the Great War was undoubtedly decisive. The change of consciousness brought about by the war could no longer tolerate the idealists' optimistic view of the universe as a harmonious order that could be expressed in a unifying narrative, whether in religious or mythical terms, or by way of philosophical and teleological schemes such as those of Hegel, which hold that history is moving toward some predetermined higher end.

2.5

One of the products of this change in consciousness was existentialism. But it is existentialism *as literature*, rather than as (merely or primarily) philosophy, that holds the greatest promise for a way out from the impasses created by both idealist thought and standard theistic philosophy (like that espoused by Hick) in the face of the problem of evil. Given its concern with concrete human existence, on both personal and political levels, existentialism *as philosophy* often tended to the expression of existentialism *as literature*, which helps explains why Sartre, Beauvoir, Camus and Marcel all made their mark as novelists and playwrights, as well as philosophers. One of their precursors, in both literary style and philosophical outlook, was the great Russian novelist and short-story writer, Fyodor Dostoyevsky. Nietzsche described Dostoyevsky as "the only psychologist...from whom I had anything to learn,"[21] and many later existentialists would echo these sentiments. What particularly fascinates readers of Dostoyevsky is his psychological acumen, his ability to delve into the dark and contradictory recesses of the human mind, a mind simultaneously attracted to the "ideal of the Madonna" and the "ideal of Sodom," as Dmitry Karamazov laments in Dostoyevsky's final novel, *The Brothers Karamazov.*[22]

As this suggests, a powerful theme running through Dostoyevsky's work is *the critique of rationalism*, one aspect of which involves the attempt to expose the dangers of 'nihilism.' This is not exactly nihilism as ordinarily understood today, as belief in nothing, or the rejection of all values, or the rejection at least of any absolute (non-relative) values or ideals such as truth and goodness. This is, rather, nihilism in a late nineteenth-century Russian context, where the term was popularized by Ivan Turgenev to describe young radicals in Tsarist Russia. In his greatest novel, *Fathers and Sons* (1862), Turgenev has the younger generation represented by two university students, Arkady and Bazarov, who reject what they perceive as their elders' romantic decadence and ineffectual politics, and who seek to swiftly, if not violently, overturn the status quo through nihilism. "The nihilist," Arkady explains to his uncle, "is a man who bows down to no authority, who takes no single principle on trust, however much respect be attached to that principle."[23] Bazarov elaborates that, in refusing to recognize any authority, "we are guided by what we recognize as useful," and "the most useful course of action at present is to reject—and we reject...everything."[24] But Bazarov's nihilism, even if incomprehensible and terrifying to the ageing gentry of the 1840s generation in Russia, doesn't quite deny *everything*, only everything associated with the *ancien régime*. In opposition to the past, and especially the Judeo-Christian past, the 'nihilistic' revolutionaries that sprang from the ranks of the *raznochintsy* in the 1860s embraced many of the prevailing Western intellectual currents of the day, including Feuerbachian atheism, materialism, feminism and British utilitarianism.

These ideas and their utopian pretensions (as illustrated, in particular, by Nikolay Chernyshevsky's novel of 1863, *What Is to Be Done?*, described as "literally the bible of the radical intelligentsia")[25] are forcefully critiqued in Dostoyevsky's novels, beginning in *Notes from Underground* (1864) and continuing in his subsequent four great 'murder' novels completed in the last fifteen years of his life. What the nihilists fail to see, according to Dostoyevsky, are that ideologies or ideals, Causes of whatever stripe, are inevitably lost causes, doomed to failure because they cannot accommodate the complexities, vagaries and frailties of life. This is why Causes often bring out the worst in people and states, justifying and legitimating terrible crimes. (Consider only the state-sanctioned evils of communism, which Dostoyevsky's novels prophetically foretold.) The revolutionaries, however, have no moral scruples: the current regime must be destroyed, at whatever cost, if a better world is to be created. Given the greatness of their ends, any means are justified to impose their political ideals on society. But the end result, for Dostoyevsky, will inevitably be far worse than what the radicals seek to overturn—and this is because the kind of rational worldview proposed by idealists and nihilists alike pays little heed to the nature of human nature, and especially its *freedom* and *irrationality*. These are the very qualities that afford us a degree of control and spontaneity, thus allowing us to withstand coercion and manipulation. They are also the qualities that make us both singular and diverse, as each person carries within them the potential to rise above the anonymous crowd and achieve individuality (or 'authenticity,' as the existentialists liked to say).

Dostoyevsky liked to employ the image of the 'anthill' to represent the kind of society envisioned by the revolutionaries. We are offered a socialist paradise, but the reality will be a dystopian environment deprived of any personal and spiritual characteristics: a homogenized order whose harmony is as specious as the anthill's, for it depends on crushing the individual and denying freedom. This becomes clear in *Demons* (1871–72), where one of the revolutionaries, Shigalyov, devotes himself to the study of the reformation of society and ends up constructing a utopian system in which the freedom of a small minority depends upon the enslavement of everyone else. Even Shigalyov concedes that this is not what one would expect an earthly paradise to look like, but there is no other option, he contends:

> I have become entangled in my own data, and my conclusion stands in direct contradiction to the initial idea from which I started. Proceeding from unlimited freedom, I end with unlimited despotism. I will add, however, that there can be no solution of the social formula except mine.[26]

There is equality here, but it is the equality of the anthill or the herd, or as a supporter of Shigalyov's scheme, Pytor Stepanovich, puts it: "All are slaves, and are equal in their slavery."[27] But the most powerful expression of Dostoyevsky's misgivings about the attempt to build and live by a rational worldview occurs in 'The Grand Inquisitor' story in *The Brothers Karamazov*. Set in sixteenth-century Seville, at the height of the Inquisition, this 'poem' told by Ivan Karamazov tells of Christ's return to earth, only to be captured and imprisoned by the Cardinal himself, the Grand Inquisitor. The Cardinal's revealing message to Christ is that the Church has rejected the burdensome freedom promised by Christ, opting instead to rule and enslave its flock by means of "miracle, mystery and authority," for (as he puts it) these are the "only three powers on the earth that are capable of eternally vanquishing and ensnaring the consciences of these feeble mutineers, for their happiness."[28] This might seem a compassionate response to the human predicament, but it is also one driven by power and lies. Just like the totalitarian Kallipolis ('ideal city') in Plato's *Republic*, founded upon a "noble lie" to convince citizens of their unequal standing and deep tie to the city (414b–415d), so too the Grand Inquisitor's Church is sustained (as Rowan Williams explains)

> by a deliberate falsehood: by the denial that freedom is anything more than the choices enabled for reasonable beings in a state of security, by the persuasion that these choices are the same as real freedom, by the appeal to a clear system of rewards and

punishments, so that moral choices are constrained by imagined consequences, and finally by the appropriation of religious rhetoric to sanction the static and controlled society that all this implies.[29]

Dostoyevsky counters the rationalist delusion not only by exposing its false foundations and its devaluation of autonomy, but also by filling his stories with the forces of irrationality, whether these be dark (madness, murder, suicide, hallucinations, addictions) or positive (love and compassion for absolutely everyone and everything). Sarah Young has insightfully put this in terms of Dostoyevsky's rejection of the prevalent tendency of his contemporaries to reduce human behaviour to materialist and mechanical explanations, thus eliminating what is perhaps most distinctively human: our unconscious and irrational impulses, our capacity to desire what we ought not to, our freedom to act in a range of damaging and destructive, and hence 'rationally' indefensible, ways.[30] Young illustrates this by emphasizing Dostoyevsky's dualism in relation to his contemporaries' monistic materialism: where they countenance only bodily surfaces, he postulates in addition

the presence of a soul or inner being…and suggests that mankind is not amenable to rational social reorganisation not only because of his irrationality, but also because the unknowability of his inner being renders it resistant to calculation, even to oneself.[31]

It is this duality, however, that unleashes the forces of light and darkness in Dostoyevsky's characters: being resistant to calculation, one's inner being can—in the appropriate circumstances—lead to great good (the compassion of Zosima), but also great evil (the criminality of Raskolnikov).

The inaccessibility of the inner being, Young further notes, is also the source of various tensions in interpersonal relationships (e.g., miscommunications, misunderstandings), as a seemingly unbridgeable gulf opens up between the self and the other, rendering the heart and mind of the other (to some degree at least) inscrutable. This, of course, is a well-known feature of Dostoyevsky's psychologically penetrating characterizations, where the dark and disunified recesses of the self turn out to be far more complicated and pathological than expected. One is reminded of the dualism between the ordinary and the fantastic in Kafka, whose bewildered and isolated protagonists also find meaning and understanding inaccessible. But where Dostoyevsky and Kafka part ways is over their response to this crisis. In Kafka, there is no redemption from alienation and absurdity, whereas a resolution is available in Dostoyevsky which allows access to the inner. As Young points out,

> While the inability to perceive beyond the outer body is the norm among Dostoevsky's characters, in particular the anti-heroes whose ideologies lead to violence, the transformative potential, for both parties, of compassion and the refusal to judge, is related to the capacity for seeing the inner being of the other, which arises from an understanding of suffering.[32]

In, for example, Prince Myshkin in *The Idiot* and especially in Elder Zosima in *The Brothers Karamazov* Dostoyevsky offers a 'way out' of the impasse in human relations, predicated upon (i) clearly 'seeing' or insightful perception of the suffering of others, and (ii) a compassionate response to that suffering, which includes (iii) a refusal to pass judgement on the other's sins, even assuming the burden of the other's sins ("in truth each of us is guilty before the others for everyone... and I thought—in truth I am perhaps more guilty than all"[33]).

2.6

Dostoyevsky's contemporary in Copenhagen, Søren Kierkegaard, provides an instructive philosophical parallel. One of the targets of Kierkegaard's polemic was the claim to 'systematicity' in post-Kantian idealism, above all in Hegel. As mentioned earlier, in Hegel there is a faith in the ultimate harmony of things, and a belief that all of human existence can be enclosed within a system. The goal of Hegel's philosophy is to construct such a system, to synthesize all knowing, thereby rendering the overall structure of reality fully intelligible from the impersonal standpoint of pure reason. That such a venture was even contemplated exposes Hegel's optimism and sympathies with Enlightenment ideals.

Kierkegaard, by contrast, regarded such claims to systematicity as both impious and comical—hence, the vitriol and satire he directed against the Hegelians. Where Hegel and his Danish followers went wrong, according to Kierkegaard, was in their *illicit identification of essence and existence, thought and reality.* As an 'experiment in thought,' Kierkegaard had no objection to Hegel's system. But when that thought was confused with reality, or when it was made the basis for deductions about reality, Kierkegaard felt Hegel's hubris had gotten the better of him. In *Concluding Unscientific Postscript* (1846),

Kierkegaard responds with a sustained satire against the idea that philosophy can be a systematic science:

> Existence itself is a system—for God, but it cannot be a system for any existing spirit. System and conclusiveness correspond to each other, but existence is the very opposite... Existence must be annulled in the eternal before the system concludes itself.[34]

In another memorable passage, perhaps influenced by Kant's famous dove metaphor, Kierkegaard continues to ridicule claims to finality and completeness:

> If a dancer could leap very high, we would admire him, but if he wanted to give the impression that he could fly—even though he could leap higher than any dancer had ever leapt before—let laughter overtake him. Leaping means to belong essentially to the earth and to respect the law of gravity so that the leap is merely the momentary, but flying means to be set free from telluric conditions, something that is reserved exclusively for winged creatures, perhaps also for inhabitants of the moon, perhaps—and perhaps that is also where the system will at long last find its true readers.[35]

Kierkegaard's point here, as Merold Westphal has observed, is essentially theological: the qualitative gap between the human and the divine is fundamental (indeed, infinite), while Hegel's system compromises or even collapses it.[36] For Hegel (as for Plato), in other words, absolute and systematic knowledge requires the transcendence of temporal existence, adopting a standpoint outside of time (*sub specie aeternitatis*); while in Kierkegaard's view, concrete existence is irreducibly temporal and finite. As Kierkegaard liked to say, "pure truth is for God alone," "existence is a system—but only for God" and (in Westphal's 'translation' of Kierkegaard) "God, but not Hegel, can be an Hegelian."[37] Kierkegaard thus insists, in yet another affirmation of Socratic ignorance, that no final or presuppositionless philosophical system can be constructed; philosophy is at best partial and perspectival.[38]

2.7

Kierkegaard has often been criticized as an irrationalist—even Albert Camus, who developed a philosophy of the absurd, was suspicious of Kierkegaard's tendency "to deify the only certainty he henceforth possesses, the irrational."[39] Camus immediately added: "The important thing, as Abbé Galiani said to Mme d'Epinay, is not to be cured, but to live with one's ailment. Kierkegaard wants to be cured."[40] To see the radicality of Camus' response, consider again Kierkegaard's slogan: "existence is a system—but only for God," or as Westphal likes to say (in response to the secular postmodern view that 'the truth is that there is no Truth'): "The truth is that there is Truth, but in our finitude and fallenness we do not have access to it."[41] From this, Westphal points out, the correct conclusion to draw is not that there is no God, but only that we are not God. There is an admission here, nonetheless, that "there is Truth," that "existence is a system," an admission entirely in line with the Hegelian perspective that the final truth is found in the whole, not in the parts (nor in any mere assemblage of the parts). What this entails, with respect to the problem of evil, is that resolution and redemption are live possibilities, if not secure certainties—even if access to the mechanics of resolution are forever beyond human understanding. Nineteenth-century Hegelians, in both Germany and Britain, were not afraid to 'systematize existence' by configuring it as an all-embracing and harmonious whole, the Absolute, a vast and eternal many-in-one. But Kierkegaard, as much as his Hegelian opponents, remains wedded to this view (or something analogous to it), as does Dostoyevsky and indeed anyone who subscribes to traditional Christian metaphysics. In rejecting such a metaphysics, what Camus (unlike Westphal) is rejecting is not merely the epistemological claim to privileged access to the way things really are. This doesn't go anywhere near far enough. What Camus above all rejects— as do others who stand in this tradition of secular existentialism, including Nietzsche and Kafka—is *the very assumption that there is a 'system.'* Not only can we not construct and live by an entirely rational system (given that our cognitive, moral and other powers are limited or distorted), but reality itself does not present itself as a 'system,' as a rational, harmonious order where all contradictions and conflicts are somehow finally resolved. There is no system, and therefore no resolution.

Jeff Malpas highlights this difference by noting Dostoyevsky's response to the dark and destructive forces residing within human nature by way of a Christian humanist ethic of love, and then contrasting this with the response to the same situation found in the stories of Franz Kafka:

> If in Dostoevsky one finds an account of the uncertainty and
> pain of the human condition that nevertheless demands of us a

human and ethical response, no matter how difficult that may be, that same condition reappears in the work of Franz Kafka in a way that emphasizes its absurdity and apparent meaninglessness, but without any sense of the same ethical response. It is as if, in Kafka's universe, no such response is even conceivable.[42]

Like Kafka, Nietzsche too refuses meaning in suffering. For example, the Christian view of suffering as having redemptive value is rejected by Nietzsche as deriving from an unhealthy 'slave morality' that is life-negating, that has been forged in the bad air of revenge, *ressentiment*, hatred, impotence, and cowardice. As Clancy Martin explains:

Nietzsche accepts as a premise what seems to be a view shared by all of the major world religions and the ancient Greek tragic view, as he understands it: life is full of suffering. The most important spiritual question, Nietzsche thinks, is how one responds to the fact of suffering life presents us with. Nietzsche sees something redemptive about suffering, but, unlike the Christian view, he does not suppose that we are redeemed by suffering: he insists that we do not need redemption, that life does not need redemption. It is our view of suffering, rather, that stands in need of redemption; that is, we must understand suffering not as an indictment of life and our living of it, but as an essential aspect of life that constitutes part of what makes life worth living. To put his view into a simple slogan, Nietzsche advocates redemption *of* suffering as a celebration and affirmation of human beings and this life, rather than redemption *by* suffering as a protest and an accusation against human beings and this life.[43]

When considering the 'problem of Job' in *The Birth of Tragedy* and elsewhere, Nietzsche's starting-point is not merely that life is full of suffering but also that suffering is without explanation, without purpose. Nietzsche to be sure claimed, as is well known, that *only as an aesthetic phenomenon is existence justified*.[44] But this is not a reversion to the theodical project of laying bare the divine blueprint for creation. Rather, Nietzsche is reverting to the tragedy-producing Greeks, who turned life into a work of art in order to make it not merely bearable but beautiful and rapturously joyful, in this way transfiguring and 'justifying' existence in full recognition of its irrational and horrific dimensions:

Here, in this supreme menace to the will, there approaches a redeeming, healing enchantress—*art*. She alone can turn these thoughts of repulsion at the horror and absurdity of existence into ideas compatible with life: these are the *sublime*—the taming of horror through art; and *comedy*—the artistic release from the repellence of the absurd.[45]

But this is not art ruled exclusively by the Apollonian disposition, which is theodical in nature in seeking redemption through dreams of order, harmony and beauty. Rather, it is art (especially the tragic dramas of Sophocles and Aeschylus) that destabilizes the Apollonian attitude with the Dionysian state of excess, intoxication and rapture, described by David Allison as

a sovereign state of exultant strength and vitality wherein existence redeems and validates itself at every moment. Hence, there is no longer any need for the redeeming vision of Apollonian beauty, the dream image of a near-forgotten Ilium, for the nostalgic hope of a long-lost kingdom before the fall, nor for submission to restrictive and tiresome codes of social order.[46]

This amounts to a profound affirmation of life in the midst of—indeed *in virtue of*—suffering. Far from offering a theodical response like Hick's, Nietzsche views life as inherently tragic and thus incompatible with any teleological scheme that renders it rationally ordered. It is for this reason that Nietzsche castigated those, like the Romantics and Schopenhauer, who sought escape into another world where there is only peace, bliss and no strife (or the absence of all willing, in Schopenhauer's case). These religious ruses are, for Nietzsche, recipes for *décadence* and nihilism, a basically hostile attitude to life, when what is needed instead is the strongest possible medicine of the joyful embrace of suffering, or *amor fati*, the 'love of fate,' the affirmation of all of life, including its evils and pains.[47]

Dostoyevsky and Kierkegaard have faith in a God for whom everything is possible, so that even the unforgivable can be forgiven, and despair ("the sickness unto death" that is the opposite of faith) need not have the last word. "The believer," writes Kierkegaard, "has the ever infallible antidote for despair—possibility."[48] For Camus, however, there is no 'antidote,' or none at least is desired: the goal is "not to be cured, but to live with one's ailment." This might seem an overly pessimistic outlook, but when asked by a journalist, "Doesn't a philosophy that insists upon the absurdity of the world run the risk of driving people to despair?", Camus responded: "Accepting the absurdity of everything around us is one step, a necessary experience: it should not become a dead end. It arouses a revolt that can become fruitful."[49] Camus expanded upon this in *The Myth of Sisyphus*, where he characterized the life lived in absurdity as a constant struggle marked by "a total absence of hope (which has nothing to do with despair), a continual rejection (which must not be confused with renunciation), and a conscious dissatisfaction (which must not be compared to immature unrest)."[50] For Camus, a life lived in lucid awareness of absurdity and the consequent lack of 'theodical' explanations for suffering does not inevitably lead to suicide. Instead, the 'absurd life' carries the potential for revolt (against the world's indifference), freedom (to shape one's life and rise above one's fate) and passion (for living for and in the present): "By the mere activity of consciousness I transform into a rule of life what was an invitation to death—and I refuse suicide."[51]

2.8

There are at least two alternative, albeit neglected, ways of expressing the same point made by atheistic existentialists without having to buy into their atheism. The first derives from a reaction to modern moral philosophy, particularly in the form of utilitarianism and deontology, and its ambition of finding the supreme principle or principles upon which all of our moral judgements can be based. In some, such as Jeremy Bentham, the project involved the construction of a moral 'rule book,' containing all the true rules of morality and all of the precise methods for applying them, including when exceptions are called for and when they are forbidden, all of which could be applied in a precise and mechanical manner. For Bentham, this was the only way out of the chaotic jumble which passed for everyday moral practice and the English legal system of the time. But as many have protested, such a hypothetical rule book is nonsensical, as morality cannot be simplified in such a way without gross distortion. The 'messiness' of morality does not allow for a simple 'moral litmus test,' a simple formula that could be used by anyone, no matter their degree of moral sophistication. Some general principles that allow for exceptions might be the best we can hope for, but anything more will fail to capture the complexity and diversity of this area of decision-making, where a certain kind of sensitivity or understanding is necessary. The idea is, of course, familiar from Aristotle, who emphasized the role of *phronesis*, or 'moral understanding,' in the achievement of a 'flourishing' life (a life of *eudaimonia*). Unlike its theoretical counterpart, *sophia*, *phronesis* is a form of 'practical wisdom' that goes beyond knowledge of facts, requiring a kind of *know-how* built upon a lifetime of training, experience and practice. This approach has been associated more recently (e.g., in the work of Bernard Williams) with an anti-codifiability or anti-theoretical view of ethics, directed against the customary goals of normative theory. Ethical phenomena, on this view, are so rich and variegated that they cannot be (faithfully) represented in a unified theory. Rather than do ethics on the model of the natural sciences, we should regard it as more like the writing of art or music criticism, where experience and judgement (often of a very personal kind) render systematization and formalization out of place.

If this anti-theoretic approach were extended to the religious or metaphysical realm, then a similar conclusion would follow: reality eludes our conceptual grasp, or (as the point is put in apophatic and mystical traditions) the infinity of the divine reality renders it 'incomprehensible': ineffable, unnameable and unknowable. For apophatic theologians, such as the fourth-century Cappadocian Gregory of Nyssa, our inability to grasp God is due not to epistemic factors such as the limitations in our cognitive capacities, but is the result of the nature of divinity itself, or more precisely the unbridgeable ontological divide (*diastema*) between Creator and creation. But if this is the case, then any attempt to construct a 'grand narrative' in the manner of a theodical explanation of evil will inevitably fail. Divinity, if not the realities of mortal life ('evil' especially), cannot be accommodated within the teleological systematization of reality involved in theodicy, where (e.g.) all evil is either 'justified' as a necessary element within the providential plan of a personal deity or 'transmuted' (in the manner of Hegel's *Aufheben*) within the all-inclusive whole that is the Absolute.

To reiterate, this is not an epistemic matter, in the manner of 'sceptical theism,' where the limits in human knowledge imply that, even if there were goods justifying God's permission of evil, it is not likely that we would discern or be cognizant of such goods. The 'failure,' rather, inheres in reality itself, thus lending the refusal of theoretical theodicy (and, by extension, sceptical theism) a certain sort of 'realism.' It is a realism that rejects as facile optimism oft-heard platitudes such as *Everything happens for a reason*, or *God (or the good) is victorious in the end*, so that any evil that takes place is always compensated or outweighed or somehow 'defeated' by God, whether in the near future or in the eschaton. Such optimism strikes many as not only false, but as perversely false in a way deserving of the scorn that Voltaire heaped on Pangloss. Bernard Williams expressed this well with respect to 'unbearable suffering':

...some suffering simply is unbearable. It can break people. This is true of physical pain, as is well known to torturers and to those who send agents into the risk of being tortured. Suffering may be such that, even when you are utterly identified with the purpose for which you are suffering, you would give *anything* for it to end. The same can be true of such things as losing a child in a struggle in which, once again, one thoroughly believes. The idea that meaning, or purpose, or understanding, or even, perhaps, a true philosophy could make all suffering bearable is a lie, whether it is told by recruiting sergeants or by ancient sages.[52]

Even a religious believer (perhaps especially a religious believer) need not deny this. What reason is there, apart from a stubborn commitment to theodicy, for thinking that there simply cannot be evil that is irrational, unjustified, irredeemable and unforgivable? Not only is it possible, but unfortunately it is very common, to identify actual evils that should forever be condemned, and that can never be redeemed or defeated, even (or especially) within a religious framework. Nothing can make amends for certain evils: it is not possible to 'undo' them so as to achieve healing and reparation. To 'gloss' such facts, in the manner of Pangloss, is to misrepresent and distort the phenomenology of tragedy.

2.9

A second route toward the rejection of the Kierkegaardian claim that 'existence, with all its joys and sorrows, constitutes a system, albeit for God only, not for humans' involves an equally metaphilosophical strategy, but a quite different one from that sketched in Section 2.8. The Kierkegaardian claim is an assumption, which the philosopher, *qua* philosopher, is not entitled to make. The idea here, one I have explored at length elsewhere,[53] is that philosophy pursued in the Socratic spirit of "going wherever the wind of the argument carries us" (*Republic* 394d), of allowing arguments and evidence to mould one's theoretical commitments, rather than complacently or dogmatically relying upon (say) the revelations of a sacred text or the authority of a religious institution, renders the very idea of a 'Christian philosophy' untenable. Philosophy that takes refuge in revelation or authority cannot but assume the form of a finished product, as possessing the ultimate answers even if their precise content or the steps required to reach them are open to debate. As Bertrand Russell remarked of Aquinas' practice in dealing with the question of the existence of God, Aquinas was always convinced of the truth of the conclusion even before the argument had gotten underway.[54] By contrast, genuinely following the argument wherever it leads means being prepared (and not merely theoretically) to give up one's most cherished commitments, where this might involve constantly beginning anew and setting off in new directions. In short, rather than an ideologically-driven philosophy that cannot easily be dislodged by reason, we are to re-envision the discipline along more sceptical (in both the 'doubtful' and 'thoughtful' senses) and adventurous lines, with a willingness to explore, test, imagine and even play, without presuming to have 'all the answers' in advance.

One might object that this is precisely the point of Kierkegaard's use of Socratic dialectics. As William McDonald has observed, Kierkegaard "needed a form of rhetoric which would force people back onto their own resources, to take responsibility for their own existential choices, and to become who they are beyond their socially imposed identities."[55] This led Kierkegaard to his use of the method of 'indirect communication,' where traditional genres of philosophical writing (e.g., the treatise or journal paper aimed at demonstrating the truth by the use of argument) give way to a more literary and polemical style, involving the use of multiple pseudonyms as well as irony, parody, satire and humour. The aim is not to directly impart some cognitive truths or facts or information, as scholarly and scientific texts seek to do, but to create the conditions necessary for the reader or audience to enter into a new, transformative and dialectical, relationship with the truth. But truth here, according to McDonald, is to be understood in terms of "practical self-knowledge, which can be communicated only by indirect means. It transforms the learner into a new self, from one state of being into a new state of being."[56] Kierkegaard's rhetorical techniques, on this view, offer not so much pre-packaged answers as certain kinds of practical capabilities, or a set of tools on how to become a 'single individual' amongst 'the crowd' and, above all, how to become a Christian in Christendom. This intentional inversion of Hegelian dialectics—a dialectics aimed at scaling the *scala paradisi* to the mind of God merely by making one's way through the stages of Hegel's 'science of logic'—was part of Kierkegaard's overall strategy of making everything more difficult, especially God and Christian faith. And this meant taking away knowledge, removing comprehension and exposing ignorance, much like Socrates and the ancient sceptics, for whom doubt was "the task of a whole lifetime."[57]

But notice how these strategies and communications are framed in Kierkegaard. The general framing principle, or working assumption, is nothing less than *the truth of Christianity*—and not just any version of Christianity, but a very specific version arising out of the Protestant Reformation and the Lutheran tradition (which means that an entire range of alternative, including 'heretical,' Christian theologies and spiritualities has been excluded). This working assumption, in Kierkegaard, is not up for serious question or doubt (after his conversion experience as a student, on 19 May 1838, did Kierkegaard ever change his mind about the truth of Christianity?), but is the basis upon which all else is subjected to question and criticism. This has the effect of reducing Kierkegaard's method of proceeding, as much as Aquinas,' to a form of 'ideology' where reality is made to fit within a fixed, pregiven schema (in this case, Lutheran Christianity) which can never be overturned.

This might seem unfair to Kierkegaard, who insists on the 'existential' character of faith as a necessarily risky affair, involving commitment (to beliefs, practices, etc.) but *without guarantees*—without any guarantees that it is not misplaced or mistaken. But even this conception of faith is conditioned by a certain way of thinking about Christianity and its demands on the individual. It is Kierkegaard's antecedent commitment to Christianity and indeed to a particular brand of Lutheran Christianity (one where seriousness, sin, suffering, guilt and individual isolation take precedence over the light, joyous, celebratory and communal aspects of Christianity) that leads him to conceive of faith as risky and passionate, as the product of "the contradiction between the infinite passion of inwardness and the objective uncertainty."[58] What Dominique Janicaud has said of the recent theological turn in French phenomenology applies just as well to earlier forms of religious existentialism: "The dice are loaded and choices made; faith rises majestically in the background."[59]

Despite Kierkegaard's intentions, a 'Christian philosophy' will never be sufficiently Socratic; a more promising, because more sceptical, way of approaching the problem of evil is necessary. This also is the diagnosis made, in her own insightful way, by Beverley Clack, in the course of seeking to counteract the traditional (e.g., theodical) response to the problem of evil with one that is 'aporetic.'[60] Borrowing from the psychoanalytic model of therapy as a 'pathless path' or *aporia*, Clack envisages the problem of evil not as an abstract or theoretical puzzle that has to be solved but as an existential journey with no predetermined goal or end-point—"a journey where the road is strange and unknown."[61] Clack's model does not look for definitive or universally applicable solutions, but encourages relentless and multifarious exploration. In line with this, greater emphasis than usual is accorded to the personal and subjective point of view (the first-person perspective). And so Clack does not hesitate to defer to the testimony of Holocaust survivors as well as to the literary and creative arts for insights into evil and suffering (something rarely done in contemporary discussions on the problem of evil), and this because "the best art challenges, forcing the viewer/reader to consider again the way in which they habitually see the world."[62] In approaching the problem in such a holistic and phenomenological manner, it is possible to explore the intellectual and emotional dimensions of evil at the same time (without drawing artificial contrasts between the two) and to empathically engage with the lived experience of suffering, allowing it to shatter and transform one's assumptions.

To achieve such a transformation, however, and to overcome the limitations of our ordinary or detached 'outsider' perspective when dealing with evil, Clack insists that our focus must shift to "*listening* to the one who is experiencing suffering at first hand. To listen means that the sufferers' experiences are less likely to be forced to cohere with any existing ideas that might be held about the nature of things."[63] The temptation to distort, to force things to cohere, is particularly strong in theodicy, where (as Clack observes) there is a tendency to 'remodel,' 'stretch' or 'mutilate' the phenomena of suffering and evil, so as to render them more compatible with one's favoured brand of theism.[64] Clack's model, by contrast, begins with the realities of evil and allows these to "shape how we subsequently understand the nature of things."[65] Kenneth Surin, in *Theology and the Problem of Evil*, similarly emphasizes the importance of allowing the experience of evil to impinge upon received religious wisdom: "If anything is Christianity's primary concern with regard to what took place at Auschwitz…it is, rather, to allow itself to be reinterpreted, to be 'ruptured,' by the pattern of events at Auschwitz."[66] On this view, as Surin states, "the Christian message will now be the *interpretandum*, the history of Auschwitz the *interpretans*."[67] Reversing the order of interpretation in this manner suggests a metaphilosophy far removed from the one advanced by Christian philosophers, whether they be existentialists or not. As Clack states: "A different model for the philosophy of religion is needed, one that is fluid, that does not seek to make all things fit neatly together but allows, in Wittgenstein's words, what is rugged to stay rugged."[68]

Again, this attempt to reclaim the subjective, first-person perspective seems precisely in keeping with Kierkegaard's emphasis on individuality and inwardness, on regarding the religious life not in terms of disinterested objectivity, but under the existential categories of risk and urgency, personal and passionate engagement. For Kierkegaard, then, evil is confronted not as a 'problem' but as a 'mystery,' to borrow Gabriel Marcel's distinction.[69] For Marcel, mysteries are not amenable to theoretical speculation or technical resolution. Rather, they demand an entirely different approach, one of personal participation and involvement, where in fact the questioner is so deeply involved in the question that to remove or modify the one is at the same time to remove or modify the other. In the realm of mystery, therefore, it is not possible to substitute one person for another without altering the question itself. This entails, of course, that there can be no universal or objective solutions when it comes to mysteries, assuming it even makes sense to think of mysteries as open to 'solutions' at all given that we are not dealing here with gaps in knowledge, as happens with 'problems.' In Marcel's view, the phenomenon of evil can profitably be discussed on an abstract level as a 'problem,' but only up to a point before the mystery is degraded and becomes merely problematic—which is what happens when the concrete experience of evil is marginalized. The only way to be faithful to this experience, according to Marcel, is to approach it as a 'mystery' by way of 'secondary reflection,' an involved and participatory form of thought that recuperates the unity of experience dissolved at the level of technical and detached analysis.

Categorizing evil as a 'mystery' in this sense, however, has the effect of rendering faith invulnerable to rational criticism. Kierkegaard is well known for his fideistic tendencies, for taking an adversarial stance toward reason and seeing reason, particularly in the form of speculative (Hegelian) philosophy, as both unnecessary and inappropriate for the religious life. Although the precise nature of Kierkegaard's fideism and 'irrationalism' continue to be contested, it is clear that he does not think of Christian faith as something that can, or ought to, be derived from reason in the form of, say, natural theology or historical scholarship. To open up faith to reason in that way would, in his view, import into religion modes of inquiry that distort the essential nature of faith. If that is the case, then it seems that he would, like Marcel, view evil as fundamentally a 'mystery' to be lived out rather than a 'problem' to be intellectually resolved. By contrast, Clack's aporetic model (or at least my appropriation of it) does not allow for such self-protective measures, which obstruct genuine questioning and thinking by beginning from a faith-commitment where one has already found what one claims to be searching for—viz., God (or truth). But if we wish to grapple with the ultimate questions of life and death, good and evil, it might help to depart once in a while from the conventional and familiar, freely roaming on roads less travelled, not knowing where we are going and not even caring. This requires an interplay of rational rigour and creative imagination, perhaps occasionally buttressed by an *epochē* or suspension of belief in order to overcome the obsession with carving out a 'position' of one's own. In short, a truly Socratic spirit in philosophy consists not only in subjecting the knowledge-claims of one's interlocutor or culture to withering critique, or even parody—but also in turning these powerful tools onto one's own beliefs and presuppositions, thus demonstrating in one's own thinking a preparedness to follow the argument wherever it leads.

2.10

My starting-point was John Hick's soul-making theodicy, as an attempt to make sense of the evils of the world within a standard theistic framework. This theodicy, Hick concedes, is powerless without an eschatology for the various evils that go unredeemed in our short lifetime. I then turned to the absolute idealist tradition in German and British philosophy, which is characterized by its rejection of the very kind of eschatology Hick desperately needs—viz., the personal postmortem survival of the individual. With the project of theodicy seemingly in ruins, what alternatives are available to absolute idealists in the face of evil? The idealist proposal, elaborated in distinct ways by Kant's German and British successors, essentially involves a return to pre-Kantian system-building, with reality depicted as a unified, universal, mind-like whole (the 'Absolute') where dualities and deformities are eventually dissolved. These pretensions to systematization, seeking to mirror reality in final or complete metaphysical systems, came under pressure in the aftermath of the Great War in certain literary quarters, epitomized best in T. S. Eliot's *Waste Land*. A similar challenge was sounded even earlier by proto-existentialists in both literature and philosophy, particularly through Dostoyevsky and Kierkegaard. But the critique of Dostoyevsky and Kierkegaard, when placed alongside the contributions made by their secular counterparts, including Nietzsche and Camus, appears insufficiently radical: the very assumption of reality as constituting a 'system' (and not simply whether we have the capacity to faithfully represent it as such) is what is at issue. Without any credible basis for this assumption, evil itself lacks any foundation—not in the sense of a 'mystery,' but more fundamentally as a lack of 'meaning.' To end, as I began, with the words of Geoffrey Hill, if there is any meaning in evil, it is perhaps found in its inherent "urge to unmake / all wrought finalities."[70]

Notes

1 Hick develops his soul-making theodicy in Part IV of *Evil and the God of Love*, 1st edn (London: Macmillan, 1966).
2 Ibid., p. 362.
3 As Timothy Sprigge puts it,

> to claim that the Absolute exists is to claim that there is a single infinite centre of experience, the Absolute itself, of which all finite centres are fragments, and that everything else which in any sense exists is either a part of it, an aspect or feature of it, or something usefully posited by one of its parts, features, or aspects.
>
> ("Bradley's Doctrine of the Absolute," in Guy Stock (ed.), *Appearance versus Reality: New Essays on Bradley's Metaphysics*, Oxford: Clarendon Press, 1998, p.197)

4 See Paul Guyer, "Absolute Idealism and the Rejection of Kantian Dualism," in Karl Ameriks (ed.), *The Cambridge Companion to German Idealism*, 2nd edn (Cambridge: Cambridge University Press, 2017), §2.1.
5 Quoted in Robert C. Solomon, *In the Spirit of Hegel: A Study of G. W. F. Hegel's 'Phenomenology of Spirit'* (New York: Oxford University Press, 1983), p.87.
6 Jeremy Dunham, Iain Hamilton Grant and Sean Watson, *Idealism: The History of a Philosophy* (Abingdon: Routledge, 2014), p.117.
7 Ibid., p.122.
8 Solomon, *In the Spirit of Hegel*, p.91.
9 Ibid., p.99.
10 Yovel makes this comment in his introduction to *Hegel's Preface to the 'Phenomenology of Spirit,'* trans. Y. Yovel (Princeton, NJ: Princeton University Press, 2005), p.45.
11 Hegel, preface to *Philosophy of Right* (originally published 1821), trans. T. M. Knox (Oxford: Clarendon Press, 1952), p.10.
12 Solomon, *In the Spirit of Hegel*, p.284.
13 Hegel, *Phenomenology of Spirit*, trans. A. V. Miller (Oxford: Oxford University Press, 1977), Preface, §11, p.6.
14 *Hegel's Philosophy of Mind, Being Part Three of the Encyclopaedia of the Philosophical Sciences (1830)*, trans. W. Wallace and A. Miller (Oxford: Oxford University Press, 1971), §564.
15 Paul Redding, "G. W. F. Hegel," in Graham Oppy and Nick Trakakis (eds), *The History of Western Philosophy of Religion* (Durham: Acumen, 2009), vol. 4, pp.59–60, emphases in original.
16 Solomon, *In the Spirit of Hegel*, p.87.
17 Ibid., pp.vii–viii.
18 Ibid., p.viii, emphasis in original.

19 The dissertation was later published by Eliot as *Knowledge and Experience in the Philosophy of F. H. Bradley* (New York: Columbia University Press, 1964).
20 Bertrand Russell, "My Mental Development," in P. A. Schilpp (ed.), *The Philosophy of Bertrand Russell* (La Salle, IL: Open Court, 1989), p.12, emphasis in the original; similarly, he elsewhere states: "It was an intense excitement, after having supposed the sensible world unreal, to be able to believe again that there really were such things as tables and chairs" (*Autobiography*, London: Unwin, 1987, p.135).
21 Friedrich Nietzsche, *Twilight of the Idols*, §45, in *Twilight of the Idols and The Anti-Christ*, trans. R. J. Hollingdale (London: Penguin, 1990), p.110. Note also Nietzsche's enthusiasm upon discovering Dostoyevsky:

> I knew nothing about Dostoevsky, not even his name, until a few weeks ago... In a bookshop my hand accidentally came to rest on *L'esprit souterrain* [comprising the novels 'The Landlady' and 'Notes from the Underground'], just recently translated into French (the same kind of chance brought me in acquaintance with Schopenhauer when I was 21, and with Stendhal when I was 35). The instinct of affinity (or what shall I call it?) spoke to me instantaneously—my joy was beyond bounds; not since my first encounter with Stendhal's *Rouge et Noir* have I known such joy.
>
> (Letter of 23 February 1887 to Franz Overbeck)

Quoted in Paolo Stellino, *Nietzsche and Dostoevsky: On the Verge of Nihilism* (Bern: Peter Lang, 2015), pp.23–4.
22 Fyodor Dostoyevsky, *The Brothers Karamazov*, trans. David McDuff (London: Penguin, 1993, originally published 1880), p.122.
23 Ivan Turgenev, *Fathers and Sons*, trans. Peter Carson (London: Penguin, 2009), p.23.
24 Ibid., p.49.
25 The description is Ronald Meyer's, in the Notes section of Dostoyevsky, *Demons*, trans. Robert A. Maguire (London: Penguin, 2008), p.799.
26 Dostoyevsky, *Demons*, p.446.
27 Ibid., p.463.
28 Dostoyevsky, *The Brothers Karamazov*, p.293.
29 Rowan Williams, *Dostoevsky: Language, Faith and Fiction* (London: Continuum, 2008), p.30.
30 Sarah J. Young, "Fyodor Dostoevsky (1821–1881): 'Fantastic Realism,'" in Michael Bell (ed.), *The Cambridge Companion to European Novelists* (Cambridge: Cambridge University Press, 2012), ch. 15.
31 Ibid., p.265.
32 Ibid., p.271.
33 Dostoyevsky, *The Brothers Karamazov*, p.343. These are the words of Elder Zosima. Note also the words of Father Tikhon to the wicked but remorseless Stavrogin in (an expurgated section of) Dostoyevsky's *Demons*: "In sinning, each person has already sinned against all, and each person is in some way guilty for another person's sin. There is no isolated sin. I am truly a great sinner, and perhaps greater than you" (p.781).
34 Søren Kierkegaard, *Concluding Unscientific Postscript to 'Philosophical Fragments,'* ed. and trans. Howard V. Hong and Edna H. Hong (Princeton, NJ: Princeton University Press, 1992), pp.118, 122.

35 Ibid., p.124.
36 Merold Westphal, "Kierkegaard and Hegel," in Alastair Hannay and Gordon D. Marino (eds), *The Cambridge Companion to Kierkegaard* (Cambridge: Cambridge University Press, 1998), ch. 4.
37 Ibid., p.117.
38 Idealist philosophers, particularly in the British tradition of idealism, were entirely aware of this problem. As John H. Muirhead pointed out,

> Green believed that a philosophy of the Absolute was one thing, an absolute philosophy quite another. 'When we have satisfied ourselves,' he had written in 1880, 'that the world in its truth or full reality is spiritual because on no other supposition is its unity explicable, we may still have to confess that a knowledge of it in its spiritual reality—such a knowledge of it as would be a knowledge of God—is impossible to us.'
> (*The Platonic Tradition in Anglo-Saxon Philosophy*, London: George Allen and Unwin, 1931, p.209)

The quotation from Green is taken from Green's review of John Caird's *Introduction to the Philosophy of Religion*.
39 Albert Camus, *The Myth of Sisyphus*, trans. Justin O'Brien (London: Penguin, 2000), p.40.
40 Ibid., pp.40–1.
41 Merold Westphal, *Overcoming Onto-theology: Toward a Postmodern Christian Faith* (New York: Fordham University Press, 2001), p.87.
42 Jeff Malpas, "Existentialism as Literature," in Steven Crowell (ed.), *The Cambridge Companion to Existentialism* (Cambridge: Cambridge University Press, 2012), p.298.
43 Clancy Martin, "Friedrich Nietzsche," in Oppy and Trakakis (eds), *The History of Western Philosophy of Religion*, vol. 4, pp.246–7, emphases in original.
44 This formula occurs twice in the first edition, and is repeated approvingly in the "Attempt at a Self-Criticism" (the preface added to the third edition in 1886). See, e.g., §24: "But this primal and difficult phenomenon of Dionysiac art is only intelligible and can only be immediately grasped through the wonderful significance of *musical dissonance:* just as music alone, placed next to the world, can give us an idea of what we might understand by 'the justification of the world as an aesthetic phenomenon'" (*The Birth of Tragedy out of the Spirit of Music*, trans. Shaun Whiteside, London: Penguin, 1993, p.115).
45 Nietzsche, *The Birth of Tragedy*, §7, p.40.
46 David B. Allison, *Reading the New Nietzsche: 'The Birth of Tragedy,' 'The Gay Science,' 'Thus Spoke Zarathustra,' and 'On the Genealogy of Morals'* (Lanham, MD: Rowman and Littlefield Publishers, 2001), p.42.
47 This principle of valuation is closely connected to Nietzsche's doctrine of 'eternal recurrence,' that every event that has ever happened, and will ever happen, is repeated eternally. The classic statement of eternal return occurs in §341 of *The Gay Science*. See also *Ecce Homo*: "My formula for greatness in a human being is *amor fati*: that one wants nothing to be other than it is, not in the future, not in the past, not in all eternity. Not merely to endure that which happens of necessity, still less to dissemble it—all idealism is untruthfulness in the face of necessity—but to *love* it…" (trans. R. J. Hollingdale, London: Penguin, 1992, 'Why I am so Clever' §10, pp.37–8).

48 Kierkegaard, *The Sickness unto Death*, trans. H. V. Hong and E. H. Hong (Princeton, NJ: Princeton University Press, 1980), p.39.
49 Camus, "Three Interviews," in *Lyrical and Critical Essays*, ed. Philip Thody, trans. Ellen Conroy Kennedy (New York: Vintage Books, 1970), p.346.
50 Camus, *The Myth of Sisyphus*, pp.34–5.
51 Ibid., p.62. Camus goes on (in pp.64–111) to describe in more concrete detail what the absurd life might look like by way of the categories of the seducer, the actor, the conqueror, and the artist, and he ends with his best-known illustration of the absurd hero: Sisyphus. In his novel, *The Outsider* (1942), Camus offers the character of Meursault as a further concrete exemplification of the absurd life.
52 Bernard Williams, "Unbearable Suffering," in *The Sense of the Past: Essays in the History of Philosophy*, ed. Myles Burnyeat (Princeton: Princeton University Press, 2006), p.334, emphasis in original.
53 See N. N. Trakakis, "Philosophy and Religious Commitment," *Sophia, 56* (2017), 605–30.
54 See Bertrand Russell, *History of Western Philosophy* (London: Routledge, 2000, originally published 1946), pp.453–4.
55 William McDonald, "Søren Kierkegaard," *The Stanford Enclycloepdia of Philosophy* (Winter 2017 Edition), §2, ed. Edward N. Zalta, URL = <https://plato.stanford.edu/archives/win2017/entries/kierkegaard/>.
56 William McDonald, "Søren Kierkegaard," in Oppy and Trakakis (eds), *The History of Western Philosophy of Religion*, vol. 4, p.182.
57 Kierkegaard, *Fear and Trembling*, trans. Alastair Hannay (Harmondsworth: Penguin, 1985), p.42.
58 Kierkegaard, *Concluding Unscientific Postscript*, p.204.
59 Dominique Janicaud, "The Theological Turn of French Phenomenology," trans. Bernard G. Prusak, in Janicaud et al. (eds), *Phenomenology and the 'Theological Turn': The French Debate* (New York: Fordham University Press, 2000), p.27. Janicaud was referring here to Levinas.
60 See Beverley Clack, "Distortion, Dishonesty and the Problem of Evil," in Hendrik M. Vroom (ed.), *Wrestling with God and with Evil: Philosophical Reflections* (Amsterdam: Rodopi, 2007), pp.197–215.
61 Ibid., p.207.
62 Ibid., pp.207–8. Specifically, Clack considers Frida Kahlo's painting, "Henry Ford Hospital or the Flying Bed" (1932), which illustrates Kahlo's response to her experience of miscarriage, and Chuck Palahniuk's novel *Lullaby* (2002), which tells the story of a grieving husband and father who believes himself responsible for the deaths of his wife and children.
63 Ibid., p.205, emphasis in original.
64 Ibid., p.199.
65 Ibid., p.205.
66 Kenneth Surin, *Theology and the Problem of Evil* (Oxford: Basil Blackwell, 1986), p.124.
67 Ibid., p.123.
68 Clack, "Distortion, Dishonesty and the Problem of Evil," p.212.
69 See Gabriel Marcel, "On the Ontological Mystery," in *The Philosophy of Existentialism*, trans. Manya Harari (New York: The Citadel Press, 1968), pp.19–20.
70 From Geoffrey Hill, *A Treatise of Civil Power* (London: Penguin, 2007), p.51.

Bibliography

Allison, D. B. *Reading the New Nietzsche: 'The Birth of Tragedy,' 'The Gay Science,' 'Thus Spoke Zarathustra,' and 'On the Genealogy of Morals'* (Lanham, MD: Rowman and Littlefield Publishers, 2001).

Bradley, F. H. *Appearance and Reality*, 1st edn (Oxford: Oxford University Press, 1893); 2nd edn, 9th impression (Oxford: Clarendon Press, 1930).

Camus, A. *Lyrical and Critical Essays*, trans. E. Conroy Kennedy, ed. P. Thody (New York: Vintage Books, 1970).

Camus, A. *The Myth of Sisyphus*, trans. J. O'Brien (London: Penguin, 2000).

Clack, B. "Distortion, Dishonesty and the Problem of Evil," in H. M. Vroom (ed.), *Wrestling with God and with Evil: Philosophical Reflections* (Amsterdam: Rodopi, 2007), pp.197–215. https://doi.org/10.1163/9789401204019_015

Dostoyevsky, F. *The Brothers Karamazov*, trans. D. McDuff (London: Penguin, 1993).

Dostoyevsky, F. *Demons*, trans. R. A. Maguire (London: Penguin, 2008).

Dunham, J., I. H. Grant and S. Watson, *Idealism: The History of a Philosophy* (Abingdon: Routledge, 2014). https://doi.org/10.4324/9781315711447

Eliot, T. S. *Knowledge and Experience in the Philosophy of F. H. Bradley* (New York: Columbia University Press, 1964).

Guyer, P. "Absolute Idealism and the Rejection of Kantian Dualism," in K. Ameriks (ed.), *The Cambridge Companion to German Idealism*, 2nd edn (Cambridge: Cambridge University Press, 2017), pp.43–64. https://doi.org/10.1017/9781316556511.005

Hegel, G. W. F. *Philosophy of Right*, trans. T. M. Knox (Oxford: Clarendon Press, 1952). https://doi.org/10.1093/actrade/9780198241287.book.1

Hegel, G. W. F. *Hegel's Philosophy of Mind, Being Part Three of the Encyclopaedia of the Philosophical Sciences (1830)*, trans. W. Wallace and A. Miller (Oxford: Oxford University Press, 1971). https://doi.org/10.1093/oseo/instance.00070637

Hegel, G. W. F. *Phenomenology of Spirit*, trans. A. V. Miller (Oxford: Oxford University Press, 1977).

Hegel, G. W. F. *Hegel's Preface to the 'Phenomenology of Spirit,'* trans. Y. Yovel (Princeton, NJ: Princeton University Press, 2005). https://doi.org/10.2307/j.ctv1s04wkf

Hick, J. *Evil and the God of Love*, 1st edn (London: Macmillan, 1966).

Hill, G. *A Treatise of Civil Power* (London: Penguin, 2007).

Janicaud, D. "The Theological Turn of French Phenomenology," trans. B. G. Prusak, in D. Janicaud *et al.* (eds), *Phenomenology and the 'Theological Turn': The French Debate* (New York: Fordham University Press, 2000), pp.1–103.

Kierkegaard, S. *The Sickness unto Death*, trans. H. V. Hong and E. H. Hong (Princeton, NJ: Princeton University Press, 1980). https://doi.org/10.1515/9781400847020

Kierkegaard, S. *Fear and Trembling*, trans. by A. Hannay (Harmondsworth: Penguin, 1985).

Kierkegaard, S. *Concluding Unscientific Postscript to 'Philosophical Fragments,'* ed. and trans. H. V. Hong and E. H. Hong (Princeton, NJ: Princeton University Press, 1992). https://doi.org/10.1515/9781400847037

Malpas, J. "Existentialism as Literature," in S. Crowell (ed.), *The Cambridge Companion to Existentialism* (Cambridge: Cambridge University Press, 2012), pp.291–321. https://doi.org/10.1017/ccol9780521513340.015

Marcel, G. "On the Ontological Mystery," in *The Philosophy of Existentialism*, trans. M. Harari (New York: The Citadel Press, 1968), pp.9–46.

Martin, C. "Friedrich Nietzsche," in G. Oppy and N. Trakakis (eds), *The History of Western Philosophy of Religion* (Durham: Acumen, 2009), vol. 4, pp.231–48. https://doi.org/10.1017/upo9781844654666.019

McDonald, W. "Søren Kierkegaard," in G. Oppy and N. Trakakis (eds), *The History of Western Philosophy of Religion* (Durham: Acumen, 2009), vol. 4, pp.175–86. https://doi.org/10.1017/upo9781844654666.014

McDonald, W. "Søren Kierkegaard," in E. N. Zalta (ed.), *The Stanford Encyclopaedia of Philosophy*, Winter 2017 edn, §2, plato.stanford.edu/archives/win2017/entries/Kierkegaard

Muirhead, J. H. *The Platonic Tradition in Anglo-Saxon Philosophy* (London: George Allen and Unwin, 1931).

Nietzsche, F. *Twilight of the Idols and The Anti-Christ*, trans. R. J. Hollingdale (London: Penguin, 1990).

Nietzsche, F. *Ecce Homo*, trans. R. J. Hollingdale (London: Penguin, 1992).

Nietzsche, F. *The Birth of Tragedy out of the Spirit of Music*, trans. S. Whiteside (London: Penguin, 1993).

Redding, P. "G. W. F. Hegel," in G. Oppy and N. Trakakis (eds), *The History of Western Philosophy of Religion* (Durham: Acumen, 2009), vol. 4, pp.49–60. https://doi.org/10.1017/upo9781844654666.005

Russell, B. *Autobiography* (London: Unwin, 1987).

Russell, B. "My Mental Development," in P. A. Schilpp (ed.), *The Philosophy of Bertrand Russell* (La Salle, IL: Open Court, 1989), pp.1–20.

Russell, B. *History of Western Philosophy* (London: Routledge, 2000).

Solomon, R. C. *In the Spirit of Hegel: A Study of G. W. F. Hegel's 'Phenomenology of Spirit'* (New York: Oxford University Press, 1983).

Sprigge, T. L. S. "Bradley's Doctrine of the Absolute," in G. Stock (ed.), *Appearance versus Reality: New Essays on Bradley's Metaphysics* (Oxford: Clarendon Press, 1998), pp.192–217.

Stellino, P. *Nietzsche and Dostoevsky: On the Verge of Nihilism* (Bern: Peter Lang, 2015). https://doi.org/10.3726/978-3-0351-0860-6

Surin, K. *Theology and the Problem of Evil* (Oxford: Basil Blackwell, 1986).

Trakakis, N. N. "Philosophy and Religious Commitment," *Sophia, 56* (2017), 605–30. https://doi.org/10.1007/s11841-017-0575-z

Turgenev, I. *Fathers and Sons*, trans. P. Carson (London: Penguin, 2009).

Westphal, M. "Kierkegaard and Hegel," in A. Hannay and G. D. Marino (eds), *The Cambridge Companion to Kierkegaard* (Cambridge: Cambridge University Press, 1998), pp.101–24. https://doi.org/10.1017/ccol0521471516.005

Westphal, M. *Overcoming Onto-Theology: Toward a Postmodern Christian Faith* (New York: Fordham University Press, 2001).

Williams, B. "Unbearable Suffering," in M. Burnyeat (ed.), *The Sense of the Past: Essays in the History of Philosophy*(Princeton, NJ: Princeton University Press, 2006), pp.331–7. https://doi.org/10.1515/9781400827107.331

Williams, R. *Dostoevsky: Language, Faith and Fiction* (London: Continuum, 2008).

Young, S. J. "Fyodor Dostoevsky (1821–1881): 'Fantastic Realism,'" in M. Bell (ed.), *The Cambridge Companion to European Novelists* (Cambridge: Cambridge University Press, 2012), pp.259–76. https://doi.org/10.1017/ccol9780521515047.017

3   Life and Finite Individuality
Revisiting a Debate in British Idealism[1]

3.1

Whenever the greatest philosophical rivals of the day have come together to debate, whether in person or on paper, the results have been less than impressive, to say the least. In recent times, these debates have often featured representatives of the so-called Continental and analytic streams of philosophy. One thinks, for example, of the encounter in the late 1970s between Derrida and Searle over speech-act theory, an encounter better characterized as a dispute than a debate, and one rife with misunderstandings and insults. The wide, almost unbridgeable, differences between them were prefigured in many ways a few years earlier, in 1971, when Michel Foucault debated Noam Chomsky, this time live on Dutch television, over the question as to whether human nature is universal or constructed, and the political implications of upholding one or the other of these views.[2] At the turn of the twentieth century, the social and intellectual landscape in the Western world looked vastly different, and when the philosophical titans of the time met to discuss what concerned them most, it was not language or politics that was at the forefront of their interchange, but metaphysics of the most arcane sort. This debate, now largely forgotten, took place in London on 7 July 1918, and was hosted by the Aristotelian Society under the title of 'Do finite individuals possess a substantive or an adjectival mode of being?'[3] The opaque terminology of this question concealed a range of issues that had been preoccupying and indeed dividing British philosophy for decades, eventually leading to a vigorous exchange between the two leading schools: personal idealism, represented by Andrew Seth Pringle-Pattison;[4] and absolute idealism, represented by Bernard Bosanquet. This may have had the trappings of an in-house squabble, but I wish to argue that the nature of the exchange and its implications were far wider. At the heart

DOI: 10.4324/9781003378624-3

of this meeting, I contend, were two competing ways of understanding the relationship between divinity and humanity, and the value and purpose of human life. And to cast light on this disagreement, I will turn to a later but parallel confrontation, that between idealism and existentialism.

3.2

Before delving into the Aristotelian Society debate, I want to briefly consider a very influential way of thinking about divinity, or God, that lies in the background of this debate. This, in short, is to think of God in personal terms, where the 'personal' dimension is modelled on our knowledge of human persons. For example, in the currently fashionable Anselmian or 'perfect-being' version of theism, a concept of God is constructed by identifying a set of so-called 'good-making' properties, or properties that it is intrinsically better to have than to lack. Such properties, it is argued, would at least include consciousness, freedom, power, benevolence and knowledge—and these are then ascribed to God, with the proviso that in God, these properties have none of the limitations or defects that customarily beset humans. God is accordingly conceived as thoroughly benevolent, infinitely knowledgeable, all-powerful, etc.—in short, as an absolutely perfect being, or as Anselm said, "that than which nothing greater can be conceived." Now, even if God is not regarded as *a person* (though he often is by philosophers working within the 'perfect-being' tradition), he is at least conceived as *personal*, given that the 'good-making' properties that go to make up his nature are at the same time 'person-making' properties: they are an intrinsic part of what it means to be a personal being. Further, it is *human* personality that is the model, or at least the starting-point, in this method: the properties ascribed to God are those we first find in us, specifically the properties that exemplify human nature at its best. And it is this that has given rise to suspicions of anthropomorphism. God, on the perfect-being model, looks much like a human being, albeit a quite extraordinary one, one inflated into infinite proportions: a "super-duper superman" (in Andrew Gleeson's words), or "the biggest thing around" (as David Burrell puts it[5]). The gulf between Creator and creatures may be great, but it is not an absolute one, for it is only one of degree. Whether this is a case of mere projection, as Feuerbach and Freud claim, or whether it is a reflection of the divine 'image and likeness' in human beings, as Christian theology teaches, is a moot point. For what matters is the continuity between the human and the divine.

It is this presumed continuity that has troubled many Christian theologians who like to emphasize the mystery and ineffability of the divine, but also many Christian philosophers influenced by the Thomist view of God as *ipsum esse subsistens*, subsistent being itself, or *actus purus*, pure act or activity. A leading proponent of the Thomist view in contemporary philosophy of religion has been the Dominican and 'analytical Thomist,' Brian Davies. He takes the doctrine of divine simplicity to constitute the core of any religiously and philosophically adequate conception of God, and he claims that this doctrine has the weight of tradition behind it:

> That God is entirely simple is a teaching that has been reiterated by generations of Christians. It is found in the writings of Augustine of Hippo, Anselm of Canterbury, and Thomas Aquinas. It was formally ratified by the Fourth Lateran Council and the First Vatican Council. No historian of Christianity can plausibly deny that it has featured significantly in Christian discourse.[6]

"Yet," he goes on to note, "recently, some Christian (and some non-Christian) analytic philosophers who have turned to the claim that God is simple have rejected it." Davies has therefore devoted much of his career to explicating and defending divine simplicity, especially as this was understood by Aquinas. The central idea in Aquinas' outlook, says Davies, is the belief in God as creator, or in Aquinas' language, God as the cause of the *esse* (existence or being) of things. This seemingly innocuous belief, Davies notes, has significant implications, for it entails that God *is not*: (i) something that owes its existence to something else (God is not created or made to exist); (ii) something material or physical (if God accounts for the being of the universe, then he cannot be something bodily); (iii) something changeable, for "change derives from something causing it, while God is the cause of the being of everything other than himself (and, therefore, of all change or coming to be)";[7] and (iv) an instance of a kind (or an 'individual'): "For, not being material, God cannot, thinks Aquinas, be thought of as being an individual belonging to a class of which there could be many different members."[8] The function of the doctrine of divine simplicity, according to Davies, is to give expression to these negations, and in particular to deny the distinction of essence (*essentia*) and existence (*esse*) in God. This distinction applies only to creatures (to objects that can be singled out as members of the universe), and so in denying this distinction the doctrine of divine simplicity preserves the essential difference between Creator and creature. What simplicity teaches, then, is not so much what God is, but what God is not, in line with the apophatic tradition of Christian theology:

> Aquinas's doctrine of divine simplicity is not offered as a *description* of God, or as an attempt to suggest that God has an *attribute* or *property* of simplicity. It is not a description since (in keeping with Aquinas's promise to note ways in which God does *not* exist) it consists entirely of negations, of attempts to say what God *cannot* be. It also is not ascribing simplicity to God as an attribute or property since it explicitly denies that, in a serious sense, God has any attributes or properties. Normally, attributes or properties can be distinguished from the things that possess them. Yet... Aquinas denies that God and his nature can be thought of as distinct. It is very important to bear all of this in mind if one's aim is to understand Aquinas on simplicity, for what his teaching amounts to is what might be called an exercise in *negative* theology. It is not concerned to paint a portrait of God. Its aim is to put up 'No Entry' signs in front of certain roads into which we might turn when trying to think about God.[9]

3.2.1

There is a certain, indeed deliberate, strangeness in Davies' 'classical theist' model. Much of Aquinas' inspiration for this way of thinking about God is derived from Aristotle, who rejected anthropomorphic views of the gods (without necessarily rejecting the existence of these gods), preferring instead to demythologize the traditional tales (*Metaphysics* XII.8.1074a38–b14, *Politics* I.2.1252b26–7) and offer in their place a more elevated conception of the divine nature as a single mind that is the ultimate cause (though not the creator) of the whole universe. This first and final cause is the unmoved mover, whose life or activity Aristotle famously characterizes as "thought thinking itself" (*Metaphysics* XII.9.1074b33–5). Clearly, the Aristotelian God is far removed from personality as we know it—as expressed, for example, in the care of a parent, the affections of a friend or lover, or more broadly in the tribulations undergone by temporally and spatially embedded mortals as they muddle their way through life. But it was Aristotle's refined divinity that was to exert the greatest influence upon the classical theist tradition, represented by the likes of Anselm and Aquinas, who followed Aristotle in thinking of God as 'pure act,' an unmoved mover that is incorporeal, immutable, impassible (passionless) and timeless.

The rejection of 'real relations' in God is a key plank in the classical theist position. For Thomists, the relations between God and the world are *one-way* relations. This means that it is not within the ability of any creature to make a difference to God. God is wholly unaffected by the world. To be sure, Aquinas allows that the relation from God to creatures is real: God makes a difference, indeed a world of difference, to us. But the relation from creatures to God is purely 'rational'—in our minds only (*Summa Theologiae* I, q13, a7). This is merely another way of saying that God is an 'unmoved mover'—God moves others, but remains unmoved by them. God is, literally, without feeling or emotion. By contrast, process theists like Alfred North Whitehead and Charles Hartshorne contend that "God is the most and best moved mover,"[10] "the great companion—the fellow-sufferer who understands,"[11] thus admitting real ('two-way') relations and hence contingency in God. This is demanded, according to Hartshorne, by divine love, which must be sensitive to the joys and sorrows of the beloved. Hartshorne contrasts his empathetic and interactive God with Anselm's God who "can give us everything, everything except the right to believe that there is one who, with infinitely subtle and appropriate sensitivity, rejoices in all our joys and sorrows in all our sorrows."[12]

The classical theist view, then, emphasizes the distinctness between God and created persons to such an extent that any person-making characteristics God may have are diluted or transformed beyond recognition. Indeed, it could be argued that many of the features of the Thomist God are logically or conceptually incompatible with personhood. Take timelessness, for example: God completely transcends time, having neither temporal location nor temporal extension. On this view, God has no past, present and future, but—in Boethius' terms—has his life "all at once" (*totum simul*).[13] But could a timeless being be a person (or personal), where to be a person (or personal) is, at a bare minimum, to have the kind of reflective self-consciousness we normally associate with ourselves? (For Descartes, mind just is the capacity for such reflection or self-awareness.) Human consciousness makes possible (or perhaps just consists in) a range of activities that are temporal in nature (e.g., planning to undertake a project, hoping to win a race), and so temporality cannot be transcended without also abolishing consciousness and, by extension, personality. As Robert Coburn has stated, in the course of a critique of the Anselmian (or classical theist) conception of God:

> Surely it is a necessary condition of anything's being a person that it should be capable (logically) of, among other things, doing at

least some of the following: remembering, anticipating, reflecting, deliberating, deciding, intending, and acting intentionally. To see that this is so one need but ask oneself whether anything which necessarily lacked all of the capacities noted would, under any conceivable circumstances, count as a person. But now an eternal being would necessarily lack all of these capacities inasmuch as their exercise by a being clearly requires that the being exist in time. After all, reflection and deliberation take time; deciding typically occurs at some time—and in any case it always makes sense to ask, "When did you (he, they, etc.) decide?"; remembering is impossible unless the being doing the remembering has a past; and so on. Hence, no eternal being, it would seem, could be a person.[14]

The Thomist, however, is unlikely to be moved, given that divine simplicity is upheld—as it is by Davies—as a refusal to model the divine on the human and as an acknowledgement of the very strangeness, if not incomprehension, alluded to by Coburn. In any case, my reason for introducing this debate amongst contemporary Christian theists (all of whom wish to uphold the notion of a personal God) is because it parallels in many ways the earlier debate amongst personal and absolute idealists (where only the former countenance personality as an ultimate feature of reality).

3.3

Beginning with the absolute idealist view, this historically reached its zenith with the philosophy of Hegel, whose idealism was motivated in part by the attempt to overcome Kantian dualism. But where Kant feared to tread, and thus strictly delimited metaphysics, Hegel rushed in to uncover the nature of real being and thus reinvigorate metaphysics, principally through the development of a monumental system of 'absolute idealism.' As noted in Section 2.3, the 'Absolute' in such systems is, formally put, the ultimate reality, that which has unconditioned existence, in the sense that it is not conditioned by (relative to, or dependent upon) anything else. This unitary reality, as explained in Section 2.3.2, is conceived by Hegel as a universal consciousness or 'spirit,' which is mind-like and rationally intelligible (indeed, reality and reason are one and the same, in his view), and is in process of self-discovery or dialectical development.

Hegel's metaphysics was to exert a great influence on British philosophers in the late nineteenth century, especially on Bradley and Bosanquet.

Assuming, like Hegel, that the universe is fundamentally mental (mind-like, or mind-derivative), Bradley embarked upon a highly speculative metaphysics that seemed to denigrate, or at least radically re-envision, our commonsense and empirical understanding of nature and finite life. In Bradley's scheme, the many contradictory 'appearances' by which we strive to explain and control the world (which include the concepts of cause, relation, space, time, as well as the self) must be eliminated and replaced by a conception of 'Reality' as a maximally inclusive and immediate 'experience' (this term signalling an important deviation from Hegel's panlogicism, by placing the pre-conceptual or non-cognitive at the heart of reality). Bosanquet, Bradley's younger contemporary by two years, developed a similar view of the Absolute.

In Bosanquet's first series of Gifford Lectures, *The Principle of Individuality and Value* (1911–12), the 'principle' of the title turns out to be nothing other than the 'Absolute.' For Bosanquet, the greater a thing's 'individuality' (defined in terms of coherence or non-contradiction, wholeness or completeness, and independence or self-sufficiency),[15] the greater its value and reality. And the perfect form of individuality (indeed, the only form of genuine individuality) is to be found in the Absolute, a comprehensive unity that embraces the entire diversity of finite things without compromising the coherence and stability of the whole. Unlike traditional theistic dualism, which introduces an infinite ontological distance between the Creator and the creation, in Bosanquet's monistic system the Absolute is entirely 'immanent,' not something above and beyond the finite world, but the totality of all finite beings, existing only in and through them. In this respect, like so many others, Bosanquet was following in the footsteps of Bradley and their esteemed teacher at Oxford, T. H. Green, who similarly rejected supernaturalism in favour of immanentism, to the chagrin of more orthodox believers. Green's 'Eternal Consciousness,' unlike the traditional God of Christianity, does not exist *a se*—does not have self-existence, or 'aseity'—but is thoroughly immanent and dependent upon the finite world and individuals. As William Mander explains, Green's Eternal Consciousness "is not something wholly *beyond* or *different* from us; rather, it is something *larger* or *wider* than us."[16] Green's motivation, as Olive Anderson observes, "was the separation of the spiritual and the supernatural... God must be sought in each person's soul, and would be found through the life of Christian love."[17] Much the same could be said of Bosanquet, though for him (as for Bradley) the Absolute is not spoken of as a personal deity—and this for much the same reason as that adumbrated by Coburn: person-making properties can have no purchase on an infinite and timeless reality.[18]

Nevertheless, this reality, for both Green and Bosanquet, is insepara-
ble from mind (or mind-dependent, or 'ideal') and is unified in such a
way that nothing is wholly separate from anything else (thus constituting a form of ontological holism).[19]

3.3.1

Given the foregoing view of reality upheld by absolute idealists, what
conception of the self emerges? Bosanquet is clear that whatever
emerges it is not an 'eliminativist' stance that abolishes the self as an
illusion. The infinite Absolute, writes Bosanquet, is that which incor-
porates, not eliminates, the finite:

> We are, broadly speaking, to enter into the idea that finite experi-
> ence, though itself defective, is neither an accidental disturbance
> of the Quiet, nor a regrettable deviation from the Perfect. The
> absolute or infinite should present itself to us as more of the finite,
> or the finite at its best, and not as its extinction. More, not in time
> nor in quantity, but in completeness, in progress along the path of
> continuity which is indicated by the nature of things. It is at bot-
> tom a logical blunder to hold as obvious truth that merely to annul
> the finite is to affirm the infinite, i.e., that merely not to be in the
> finite world is logically and *per se* a presumable gain.[20]

But even if the self is not extinguished within the Absolute, Bosanquet does think it necessary to jettison some common misconceptions
about the self, particularly what he calls

> ...a quite unreally hypostasised notion of the consciousness of
> finite minds, whether of the animal or of the human type. We seem
> unable to shake off the superstition which regards them as sub-
> stances, crystal nuclei, fallen or celestial angels, or both at once.[21]

Lacking substantive being, finite consciousness cannot be considered ultimate: "its existence, as an existence, bears the unmistakeable
stamp of the fragmentary and the provisional."[22] But although not
ultimate, and indeed defective and incomplete, the finite individual
can overcome its internal discord and disharmony by a process of
self-transcendence and self-surrender:

> ...the finite being cannot attain perfection in itself, for finiteness
> excludes perfection. Of this, surely, fact and observation allow

no doubt whatever. The only way is, to abandon the pretension to perfection as a finite individual, and to claim it in virtue of absorption of heart and will in a greater being.[23]

It is by such a process of 'absorption' that the best in the self can be brought out. Idealists of the time found support in this view from the paradoxical Pauline dictum of 'dying to live' (Philippians 1:21) as well as Jesus' related saying that one must lose one's life in order to find it (Matthew 10:39, 16:25, Mark 8:35, Luke 9:24, John 12:25). Bosanquet puts this by saying that "it is only in a will above my own that I can find my own will and my freedom and independence... it is only by acknowledging myself adjectival and under necessity that I can become substantive and free."[24] To illustrate the point, Bosanquet (like John Hick after him) defers to John Keats' metaphor of the world as a 'vale of soul-making,' so as to emphasize that self-transcendence is only made possible within the context of obstacles and challenges to the claims and desires of the self, thus necessitating a world of both good and evil, pain and pleasure.[25] For Bosanquet, however, the self reaches its telos only when it has relinquished its separateness, exclusivity and even 'personality':

> So individuality, the principle of reality and the consistent whole, takes us on beyond personality in the strict sense, beyond the consciousness of self which is mediated by an opposing not-self, into the region where we go out of the self and into it by the same movement, in the quasi-religion of social unity, in knowledge, art, and in religion proper. And in all these experiences, as the repellent self-consciousness diminishes, and the sense of unity with the world and with man becomes pre-eminent—in all these individuality is strengthened, and the self, though less in opposition to a not-self, is more itself, and is more at home.[26]

The individual, then, attains maximal individuality not by insisting on its exclusive interests or atomistic character, but in going beyond its own sphere of concern and identifying with something wider, as happens in the highest forms of knowledge, art and religion.

At least one difficulty with this account, which Pringle-Pattison will make much of, concerns the end-point of the soul-making process. For it seems that the process, far from fashioning 'souls' or selves, only ends up destroying them by transmuting them into absolute experience. Bosanquet even appears to concede this, in passages such as the following, when talking of the ways in which the self is profoundly transformed in the process of moving toward the Absolute:

> As experienced in the absolute experience, when the essence of perfection is to transmute and to triumph over imperfection, it [the finite self] would no longer, so the indication runs,[27] be called a self. As we have seen and shall see, its substance would lend itself to new arrangements, to the constitution of new worlds in continuity and readjustment with other selves, *so that the experience would be no longer describable as constituting a system of selves.*[28]

But if the Absolute is not constituted by 'a system of selves,' then where have these selves gone? It seems they have been absorbed like drops of water into the limitless ocean, an analogy common in monistic (or 'non-dual') religious traditions like the Advaita Vedanta school of Hinduism, which hold to the essential identity of Brahman with our true, unqualified and unchanging self (*atman*). *Tat tvam asi,* "you [atman] are that [Brahman]," a father teaches his son in a famous dialogue in the *Chandogya Upanishad,* as the son dissolves salt in water.[29] Does the self, in Bosanquet's system, similarly dissolve and disappear within the Absolute?

If, however, we are looking for analogues to Bosanquet's 'self,' the Hindu 'atman' would be a poor choice. A far better candidate would be the very rival to the Hindu view—the Buddhist doctrine of 'no-self' and its denial of the sort of perfect, permanent and partless entity denoted not only by the notion of 'atman' but also by the 'soul' in Platonic philosophy and Christian theology. For Buddhists, what is conventionally named 'the self' is nothing more than a forever changing combination of five aggregates or elements (*skandhas*), much like Hume's (possibly Buddhist-inspired) view that "the mind is a kind of theatre, where several perceptions successively make their appearance; pass, re-pass, glide away, and mingle in an infinite variety of postures and situations."[30] For both Hume and the Buddhist, our inner experience is one of pervasive flux and change without permanence. The experience of impermanence or momentariness (*anicca*) is indeed a central plank in the Buddhist conception of the self. Nothing (or nothing in mental life) persists for more than an instant: all is transitory. But if each individual is subject to constant change, so that the elements that go to make up that person are never the same, then they have no permanent, underlying essence—'no self.' Or, as Buddhists put it, everything is characterized by 'emptiness' (*sunyata*), by the lack of substantiality—i.e., a permanent, abiding essence or intrinsic nature. And things and persons are empty in this sense because their existence is relative to, or dependent upon, various causes and conditions. In other words, the denial of the self is not simply the rejection of permanence but also the rejection of independence, the assumption that the self exists autonomously, in an independent, self-standing or 'absolute' way. This is the doctrine of 'dependent origination' (*paticca-samuppada*), which is regarded as the fundamental insight of Buddhism, illuminating the true nature of existence. The world is here pictured as a dynamic, ever-changing system where all phenomena are interconnected by relationships of mutual causality. A close parallel in Western philosophy is *process metaphysics*, where the world consists not of beings or things (e.g., Cartesian substances), but of 'processes,' events interconnected with other events and in constant change in every respect. The self, by extension, is not a persistent, distinct and unified substance (e.g., Descartes' *res cogitans*), but a nexus of continuous, interacting processes that are not entirely separate from other processes and that are wholly situated within the temporal flow and so always in a state of becoming.[31] To phrase this in Bosanquet's language from the Aristotelian Society debate, the being of the (finite) self is adjectival or predicative, not basic or fundamental like Aristotelian primary substances (*prôtai ousiai*) but derivative from and dependent upon the wider and infinite systematic whole which bestows upon it whatever (provisional or pragmatic) reality and identity it has. In Bosanquet's vision, there is only one true 'individual,' Reality or the Absolute, so that all finite things are turned into predicates of this single ultimate subject.[32]

3.3.2

In *Hegelianism and Personality* (first published in 1887), Pringle-Pattison was concerned with Hegelianism's tendency, as he saw it, of diminishing the value and reality of personhood and particularity by subsuming them within the categories of the universal and the absolute. Against Hegel and his followers, Pringle-Pattison insists on the autonomy and distinctness of the finite will, even in relation to the divine:

> The radical error both of Hegelianism and of the allied English doctrine I take to be the identification of the human and the divine self-consciousness, or, to put it more broadly, the unification of consciousness in a single Self.[33]

For though selfhood...involves a duality in unity, and is describable as subject-object, it is none the less true that each Self is a unique existence, which is perfectly *impervious*, if I may so speak, to other selves—impervious in a fashion of which the impenetrability of matter is a faint analogue.[34]

> I have a centre of my own—a will of my own—which no one shares with me or can share—a centre which I maintain even in my dealings with God Himself. For it is eminently false to say that I put off, or can put off, my personality here.[35]

Strong language indeed, which could be said to have provoked the first rupture within the British idealist movement. Pringle-Pattison was in any case to temper his language in later years. In, for example, his 1917 work, *The Idea of God in the Light of Recent Philosophy* (based upon his Gifford Lectures of 1912–13), he makes his principal target Bosanquet's account of the 'status' of the finite individual,[36] but nonetheless agrees with Bosanquet's rejection of the abstract, atomistic conception of the self,[37] acknowledging that

> it is certainly true that it is only by a convenient (though often misleading) abstraction that we can discuss the nature and conduct of the individual apart from the social whole in which he is, as it were, imbedded, and of which he appears to be the product. And as the individual is organic to society, so in still larger philosophical reference the individual is organic to a universal life or world, of which he is similarly a focus, an organ or expression.[38]

The relational nature of personal identity (nicely captured by a mobile phone slogan: "I am who I am because of everyone")[39] was to become an important strand running through much of British idealist thought, but this is where the commonality between Pringle-Pattison and Bosanquet ends.

Just as in standard theistic metaphysics, the personal idealism of Pringle-Pattison posits personality (and, by extension, the distinctness and uniqueness of human persons) as a fundamental feature of reality, rather than (as in Bosanquet) a limitation or defect to be overcome.[40] In Pringle-Pattison's view, whatever commonality two persons may share with one another, "they remain two minds to the end of the chapter, ...separate and exclusive focalizations of a common universe."[41] Bosanquet, to be sure, does not deny the obvious distinctions amongst finite individuals, but these differences are in his eyes provisional and ultimately unimportant, if not unfortunate—hence his emphasis on transcending finiteness and personality by a process of expansion of the self through blending or merging with the Absolute.[42] Pringle-Pattison sees this as inconsistent with Bosanquet's own soul-making theory, for if finite souls are a negligible or dispensable phenomenon, if what really matters and what solely survives are values and not persons, then why does the universe go to such great lengths to make and sustain persons?[43] Indeed, the very existence of the finite world becomes a mystery or brute fact in Bosanquet's scheme.[44]

In opposition to Bosanquet's monistic tendencies, Pringle-Pattison holds that "every individual is a unique nature, a little world of content which…is nowhere exactly repeated."[45] The finite individual, on this view, permanently preserves its identity as it makes its contribution to the life of the whole, whereas in Bosanquet "the finite individual is represented as yielding its contribution like a perfume exhaled in the very dissolution of its private being."[46] Returning, then, to the central question, of "whether finite individuals possess a substantive or an adjectival mode of being,"[47] Bosanquet's view—that the finite individual is not a 'substance,' *in the Aristotelian (or Spinozistic) sense* (denoting self-subsistence and independence), and hence not a 'true individual'—is rejected by Pringle-Pattison as an evasion.[48] For, according to Pringle-Pattison, this is not the kind of individuality that is at issue. The finite self is clearly not an 'individual' in the Aristotelian sense, but there remains a significant sense of individuality that Bosanquent's theory cannot countenance—viz., the self as a unique centre of immediate experience, as a "concrete thisness," existing as a 'this' or 'one' (i.e., numerically distinct) and not merely a 'what.'[49] It is "the concrete texture of existence,"[50] the subjective or first-person point of view ('what-it-is-like-to-be-me'), that Pringle-Pattison finds sorely missing in (what he regards as) Bosanquet's overly formal, abstract account of individuality as "a conflux of universals or qualities." To such accounts, Pringle-Pattison responds that "it is a trite observation that no number of abstract universals flocking together can give you the concretely existing individual."[51]

The monism of Bradley and Bosanquet is diagnosed by Pringle-Pattison as arising from their desire to deny the unmediated pluralism of 'unrelated reals.'[52] But for Pringle-Pattison, monism and pluralism are not the only options, and so he seeks to carve out a middle way, where both the infinite and the finite are treated as real and irreducible. "What I wish to contend," he writes,

> is that the existence of such [finite] centres is a fact as true and important 'from the side of the Absolute' as from the point of view

of the finite beings themselves—nay, that this differentiation or creation (according as we name it) constitutes the very essence and open secret of the Absolute Life.[53]

I will turn shortly to Bosanquet's response to Pringle-Pattison and, more broadly, to the matter of how this dispute could profitably be adjudicated. But first, it might be worth briefly considering another, better known, dispute which could help situate the intra-idealist controversy in a new light.

3.4

Pringle-Pattison's encounter in 1917 with Bosanquet replicates in certain ways the encounter between idealism and existentialism that began with Kierkegaard's polemics against Hegel and was continued into the twentieth century by a range of French and German existentialist thinkers. Like Pringle-Pattison, the existentialists were concerned with the implications that a strong social conception of the self had for individuality and allied notions, particularly freedom and responsibility. If the nature of the self is constituted by its social context, so that the self can fully realize its potential only by relating properly to the social whole or common good (or, in Bradley's view, by acting in accordance with 'my station and its duties'),[54] then there seems to be no prospect of the individual rising above or against what Hegel called 'social morality' (*Sittlichkeit*), the ethical norms embodied in the customs and institutions of one's society.[55] For existentialists, such deference to society or the expectations of others is a sure sign of 'bad faith' and 'inauthenticity'—the attempted evasion of responsibility. These evasions or 'alibis' are quite common, if not our default setting, but they need to be seen for what they are: the abandonment of subjectivity and the very qualities that make existence unique. In Sartrean terms, what makes subjectivity or consciousness ('being-for-itself,' *l'être-pour-soir*) unique is its 'nothingness,' its fluidity, emptiness and incompleteness, its lack of being or a fixed essence—all of which is the precondition for making something of ourselves by rising to a committed, engaged, meaningful life.

Selfhood or individuality, on this view, is not substantial but 'performative': identity is something we create and enact, rather than it being imposed or determined by, say, God or nature. As Sartre put it, "man is…nothing else but the sum of his actions, nothing else but what his life is."[56] This follows from the Sartrean thesis that 'existence precedes essence,' meaning that authenticity is *achieved*, not pre-given, and it is achieved by transcending our almost-natural condition of alienation amongst the 'crowd.' Even if, as idealists hold, subjectivity necessarily involves reciprocity, and the individual is intrinsically linked to the social, this might well be something to lament, not celebrate: "Hell is other people," Sartre wrote towards the end of his play, *No Exit*.[57] Despite the title of the play, however, there is a way out: social reality as a space of enduring conflict between subjectivities, and more broadly our 'facticity' or the 'givens' of our situation (the facts about ourselves which we have not chosen or cannot be changed—e.g., our time and place of birth, our past), can be surpassed through the choices and actions we freely make.[58] Existentialism, then, is unsparing in its criticism of social life and the ways in which the 'herd' or the 'they' disguise our radical individuality—radical because of its thoroughgoing contingency. There are no final justifications or ultimate foundations (for existence and for choices), such as those that might be supplied by the idealist's Absolute. Instead, existence is experienced as 'absurd,' lacking reason and purpose, even nauseating and distressing. And this each person must face alone, without fleeing into the hands of others, or playing the part of (e.g.) a waiter, a professor, etc. and thus objectifying oneself as having a prescribed character or role. This means becoming aware of some difficult existential truths, in particular the fundamentally free-floating, fragile, insecure and angst-ridden nature of the self. It also means no longer thoughtlessly transferring responsibility to some external (e.g., political, ecclesiastical) authority, but taking ownership of one's destiny and forging one's own path, without authoritative guidance or guaranteed answers. As demanding as this might be, it makes possible a life of (genuine) freedom, authenticity and integrity—not the idealist's integrity discovered in a predetermined whole, but that represented by an identity I choose and commit myself to as my own. This, in short, is the basis of Sartre's dictum (what Thomas Flynn has called the "the maxim of Sartrean humanism")[59] that "a man can always make something out of what is made of him."[60] Even when Sartre's later work becomes increasingly politicized and seeks to reconcile existentialism with Marxism, the social ontology that is developed and the newfound emphasis given to structural causality never overtake (though they may reinterpret) the vintage existentialist value of individual responsibility.[61]

3.5

One, often overlooked, way of working through the disagreements between idealism and existentialism, as well as those amongst the two idealist schools themselves, is to examine the perspective each brings to bear on what might be called the 'destiny' of the individual. In particular, what (according to each school) becomes of the individual after death? And what does this reveal about the place of mortality and finitude in each system of thought, as well as the value and reality accorded to the individual? Reconsidering matters from the perspective of the destiny and afterlife of the individual will not necessarily resolve the differences, but it might at least throw into relief where the crucial differences lie.

3.5.1

In an essay entitled "Unvisited Tombs," Bosanquet turns (in Section 3 of the essay) to the subject of the afterlife. He acknowledges the common desire for an afterlife so that one may 'complete one's work,' but he dislikes the individualistic tenor of this desire, as it fails to take into account the fact that works or projects are never undertaken and completed in isolation:

> The student or statesman who longs for a continuance in which he may "complete his work"—some task in the universe analogous to his function on earth, is thinking mainly of those high values of which great individuals are the vehicle. One dares not say that he is wrong; but the consideration of the vast masses of humanity suggests supplementary ideas. If not the pre-eminent, yet the widest work of the world is nameless, general, indivisible. To the student who uttered his desire to complete his work elsewhere some of us would hold it natural to answer, "But no man completes his work himself."[62]

Bosanquet goes on to discuss some of the implications for personal postmortem survival, given a holistic view of reality, or "the general indivisible spirit of things."[63] If reality is organically unified in such a way that the finite individual is destined to become absorbed into the infinite whole, this need not undermine or jeopardize their contributions to 'soul-making' while on earth. Even after the person has passed away, their contributions continue, albeit in transformed form:

> To any one strongly influenced by reflections like these, the ending of life on earth presents itself not quite as it did to the student whom we imagined above. Such a one is undogmatic as to what may come, but he needs no primary reliance on individual

survival as instrumental to continuing or completing in his own person his earthly functions or their analogue. He does not even feel that he is losing hold on his work, and preparing to bequeath it to a successor, either another on earth or himself in a new life. Rather it seems to him to be resuming its absorption in the general thought and effort of the world, from which, as ascribed to some one worker, it was discriminated for a time only, and that most arbitrarily and superficially. It is passing away on every side, he feels, not by death and destruction, but by transformation into kindred forms of the spirit through which the unity of things affirms itself in humanity.[64]

Upon death, one merges into the wider current of life—one becomes "nameless."[65] Taking his cues from the ending of George Eliot's *Middlemarch*, where Eliot states that the fortunate condition of the world, or of an individual's life, rests to some extent with "the number who lived faithfully a hidden life, and rest in unvisited tombs," Bosanquet makes the point that what matters most is not individual achievement and permanence, but the communal goods and universal values that have been realized through personal sacrifice. The person who comes to see his efforts from this broader vantage point, Bosanquet says in concluding his essay,

> does not feel himself to be dying, but to be re-living at countless points in a new life, infinitely greater than his own. Nearly all mankind rest in unvisited tombs, and leave behind them a common undistinguished work, and it is the value of this general life that we have been trying to appreciate and aspiring to share.[66]

This way of thinking of the finite individual as having only a provisional, not ultimate, value and reality is closely connected with Bosanquet's conception of identity as lateral and relational. On this holistic view of identity, the nature of the self is constituted by its entanglement in diverse networks of relations within wider wholes (e.g., family, church, state, and finally the universe itself). Early in *The Value and Destiny of the Individual*, Bosanquet puts this in teleological terms by speaking of the self's inherent 'nisus' towards unity and completion:

> What is certain, and what matters to us, is that the finite self is plainly a partial world, yet possesses within it the principle of infinity, taken in the sense of the nisus towards absolute unity and

self-completion. It is both a concentration of externality and a fragment of the Absolute.[67]

The (true) nature of the finite self, then, is given in what it may become, the self at its best and fullest. Somewhat paradoxically, self-realization is achieved in self-transcendence, in a process where the incoherence and instability of the isolated and limited self are transmuted and harmonized with higher (more vital and more perfect) wholes of experience, and eventually with the Absolute. This process of the self finding its fulfilment in the other is made possible by the 'confluence' of selves—a degree of fluidity and overlap, if not underlying unity, between them.[68] Identity, therefore, need not be restricted to literal or numerical identity, as it commonly is, but may also encompass *lateral* (or relational) identity: an identity grounded in interrelation with others, as happens (e.g.) in the coming together of individuals in a community, forming what Bosanquet calls 'a communal mind' or (borrowing from Rousseau) 'the general will.'[69]

One may wonder what, if anything, remains of finite individuality once its development is complete: is it entirely absorbed and extinguished in the Absolute? The answer lies in part in Bosanquet's conception of the Absolute, which (like Bradley's) is a unity-in-difference, rather than a homogeneous Parmenidean One. Bosanquet's monism thus makes room for plurality, insofar as the distinct contributions made by finite individuals to the whole are preserved and not annulled. The infinite whole, the Absolute, is characterized by Bosanquet as a 'world' or 'cosmos,' not a mere 'class,' and "it takes all sorts to make a world; a class is essentially of one sort only."[70] The unity of the world, as a 'concrete universal,' is best served by diversity of content: "a macrocosm constituted by microcosms."[71] The distinctive content of each microcosm or finite self, however, is predicated on the self's active and cooperative participation in the wider communities of experience in which it is sustained, and through which it grows and expands. This provides Bosanquet with a relatively robust and positive conception of the self as something which achieves its own unique particularity through a process of mutual recognition. On this view, as Avital Simhony notes, the finite self is not dissolved within some higher, communal Self, nor is it realized in negative or oppositional terms ('self-against-self'), but rather finds itself in the other: 'selves-through-selves.'[72] Simhony calls this 'strong relationality' (or 'ontological relationality'), which is not a matter of fundamentally separate individuals acting upon one another in various ways (as in 'weak relationality') but of individuals whose identity and properties are constituted by a complex web of connections.[73]

It remains the case, nonetheless, that for Bosanquet the finite self as it exists in its 'ordinary' form, prior to its purification in the fires of 'soul-making,' is not what lasts in the long run and is not what truly matters. As Bosanquet put it to Pringle-Pattison in their Aristotelian Society debate: "I cannot believe that the supreme end of the Absolute is to give rise to beings such as I experience myself to be."[74] There might be traces of the finite self that survive, in the form perhaps of a unique contribution to the whole, but within that whole the self itself has vanished, as Bosanquet admits towards the end of his paper:

> While we serve as units, to speak the language of appearance, the Absolute lives in us a little, and for a little time; when its life demands our existence no longer, we yet blend with it as the pervading features or characters, which we were needed for a passing moment to emphasise, and in which our reality enriches the universe.[75]

However, that individual souls or persons do not survive death does not entail that they lack value:

> There is no reason for denying value to minds or spirits, such as cannot, as they stand, reasonably claim survival. Perhaps, indeed, as they stand, no spirits can. It is enough that in them, in their power and impotence, their achievements and limitations, the absolute which acts in them sustains and expresses its being like the poet's mind in a drama.[76]

What counts is that the ideals we cherish most have been furthered by our efforts, even if we do not survive to see them fulfilled, like "a patriot who dies knowing that his country's freedom is secure, or...a man of science who passes away, confidently assured that the truth for which he has spent himself is victorious."[77] The philosophy of the Absolute, therefore, preserves what matters most in the common desire for immortality without having to commit itself to personal postmortem survival:

> In general, we know that what we care for, in so far as it is really what we care for, is safe through its continuity with the Eternal. In this assurance there is comprised, in principle, all that we long for in the desire for our own survival.[78]

3.5.2

Nonpersonal conceptions of immortality like this left Pringle-Pattison unpersuaded. In the closing pages of *Hegelianism and Personality*, he finds that the Hegelian system is "as ambiguous on the question of man's immortality as on that of the personality of God, and for precisely the same reason—namely, because the Self of which assertions are made in the theory is not a real but a logical self."[79] This, at bottom, is the same charge of abstraction that Pringle-Pattison was to level later at Bosanquet. Immortality, in absolute idealism, is predicated not so much of individual persons but of "the Absolute Ego, or the unity of self-consciousness as such."[80] And the Ego is immortal either because it is beyond time, or because it is the necessary presupposition of thought and existence—either way, however, "the immortality thus guaranteed can be of no concrete concern to us."[81] As Pringle-Pattison was to explain, in reference to both Hegel and Aristotle:

> the Absolute Ego or the Active Reason is in itself a pure abstraction; and to be told that we survive in that form is no whit more consoling than to be told that the chemical elements of our body will survive in new transformations.[82]

Not only does the rejection of immortality fail to provide consolation, but it also fails to cohere with the dignity and worth of human persons and, more broadly, with the moral order of the world:

> I do not think that immortality can be demonstrated by philosophy; but certainly to a philosophy founding upon self-consciousness, and especially upon the moral consciousness, it must seem incredible that the successive generations should be thus used up and cast aside—as if character were not the only lasting product and the only valuable result of time.[83]

> ... And the denial of immortality seems so much at variance with our notions of the moral reasonableness of the world, that I believe it must ultimately act as a corrosive scepticism upon morality itself.[84]

To avoid these consequences, Pringle-Pattison insisted on the irreducibility of individuality, both human and divine. As he was to put it in *The Idea of God*,

> every individual is a unique nature, a little world of content which, as to its ingredients, the tempering of the elements and

the systematic structure of the whole, constitutes an expression or focalization of the universe which is nowhere exactly repeated.[85]

This is not to endorse the view, as Bosanquet supposes, "that the supreme end of the Absolute is to give rise to beings such as I experience myself to be." The goal of soul-making, rather, is the transformation of persons into the best they can be, or as Pringle-Pattison expresses it:

> it is the spirit as God knows it and intends it to become, the spirit with its infinite potentialities and aspirations and *the consciousness of its own imperfections*, which is the fulcrum of its advance and the guarantee of a nobler future.[86]

Bosanquet, according to Pringle-Pattison, makes the mistake of conceiving the desire for personal immortality as either a desire for the survival of the self as it currently stands, "in all its poverty and meanness,"[87] or else as a desire to surrender one's self by dissolution into the Absolute. "Surely, this is to misread the situation," Pringle-Pattison responds. "Because I desire to be made more and more in the likeness of God, I do not therefore desire to *be* God."[88] Bosanquet's conception of the eventual dissolution or extinction of the finite self thus undermines, according to Pringle-Pattison, the inherent value of such individuals:

> The existence of an individual centre of knowledge and feeling is, in itself, an enrichment of the universe; and the clearer and intenser the flame of the individual life, the greater proportionally the enrichment. To merge or blend such centres is simply to put out the lights one by one.[89]

In adopting such an outlook, Pringle-Pattison takes as his starting-point a particular variety of personal theism: it is on this basis that he develops his understanding of human nature and, by extension, human destiny in the afterlife.[90] His version of theism, however, is quite unorthodox, as he himself attests. In *The Idea of God*, he argues that a transformation in the traditional understanding of God is necessary. What specifically needs to be overturned is the view of God as 'despot' (the primitive monarchical ideal) and as 'scholar' (Aristotle's eternal thinker), a conception of the deity as having a self-centred life and, as a result, an aloofness from the world.[91] A better alternative is suggested by the Christian doctrines of the Incarnation and Trinity, which (when properly understood) express the indwelling of God in humanity.[92] If, as mentioned earlier, the secret of Christianity for idealists lies in 'dying to live,' or self-sacrifice as the precondition for self-realization, then this also has consequences for how we think about the being of God. In language reminiscent of process theology (or, his critics might say, of pantheism),[93] Pringle-Pattison sums up what he calls "the open secret of the universe" as follows:

...no God, or Absolute, existing in solitary bliss and perfection, but a God who lives in the perpetual giving of himself, who shares the life of his finite creatures, bearing in and with them the whole burden of their finitude, their sinful wanderings and sorrows, and the suffering without which they cannot be made perfect. It is the fundamental structure of reality which we are seeking to determine.[94]

If the lineaments of reality are determined by the nature of divinity, then insofar as the divine is in some sense at least personal ("by the existence of the personality of God...we mean that the universe is to be thought of, in the last resort, as an Experience and not as an abstract content"),[95] the personality and individuality of human beings cannot be reduced or eliminated, whether here or hereafter. This need not mean thinking of the finite self in atomistic fashion as a fully self-contained unit—a conception which, as we saw, Pringle-Pattison rejects as much as Bosanquet.[96] But while Bosanquet (after Bradley) speaks of finite existence as a defect, limitation or appearance to be overcome or 'sublated,' Pringle-Pattison sees it as an irreducible feature of reality, integrally related to the process of divine 'kenosis':

Individuation is the very method, it may be said, of creation: without it there would be no finite world at all. And the existence of a finite world is not to be thought of as something that just happens to the Absolute, or develops itself within the Absolute only to be 'suppressed' again, 'merged' or 'absorbed.' On the contrary, the finite world is part of the inherent structure of reality. It is a process into which God pours his own life and receives it again with interest. And individuation is the method of the process, an individuation growing in distinctness and independence till it culminates in the self-conscious spirit of man, who, just because he has his own *locus* of existence, can enter into communion with his fellows and with his creative Source.[97]

In *The Idea of Immortality* (the source of the above quotation), Pringle-Pattison defends personal immortality from various criticisms put forward by Bosanquet, who regards the belief in personal survival as tied to an *irreligious* attitude towards the universe. And it is irreligious, he thinks, in part because it is selfish, whereas religion is essentially a life of sacrifice and surrender. There is nothing new, of course, in such a charge. But Pringle-Pattison responds that

> the type of experience to which it [the doctrine of personal immortality] points, so far from exhibiting preoccupation with self, is of a kind in which explicit consciousness of self may be said to disappear in the absorbing consciousness of the object.[98]

Relationships of love are a case in point: "The lover has no eyes but for his mistress, no thoughts but of her: the deeper and the purer his passion, the more is this the case. So it is with the love of God."[99] But despite being absorbed by the beloved, the lover remains a distinct individual. Without such distinctness and difference, the very love-relationship would not be possible:

> It takes two not only to make a bargain; it takes two to love and to be loved, two to worship and to be worshipped... Surely, as the poet says, sweet love were slain could difference be abolished; the most self-effacing love but ministers to the intensity of a double fruition.[100]

Taking the point regarding absorption a step further, Pringle-Pattison underscores the misleading nature of the terms believers (mystics especially) often employ to express their intimacy with God. In entering into relationship, even union, with the divine, the human person's existence (i.e., their numerical identity) is not annulled. As Pringle-Pattison puts it:

> I think it is important to realize the completely illusory character of all vague talk about merging and reabsorption. When Schleiermacher tries to comfort the mourning widow by telling her that "melting away into the great All" should be thought of as "a merging not into death but into life, and that the highest life," his words have no meaning unless the living self survives to realize the fruition of the union.[101]

Pringle-Pattison finds that even advocates of personal immortality, such as Tennyson (the Victorian poet) and Troeltsch (the

German theologian), lapse into talk of 'merging' and 'absorption,' surreptitiously introducing these terms on the basis of material analogies:

> Underlying Troeltsch's phraseology there seems to be the material metaphor of pouring or transfusing the divine essence into the individual soul as into a finite vessel, which at a given point in the process is inevitably shivered to pieces by the expanding content. But a process of growth in knowledge and spiritual communion cannot be so conceived, and the catastrophic conclusion [the annihilation of the personal self] is no more appropriate at the end of many lives than at the end of one.[102]

In his concluding lecture in *The Idea of Immortality*, Pringle-Pattison returns to Bosanquet's claim that what we really care for is preserved in nonpersonal forms of immortality, that what has lasting value are universals (e.g., goodness) rather than particulars (e.g., this good person). In spirited language, perhaps reflecting his experience of losing his youngest son in action in 1916, Pringle-Pattison rejects any conception of persons that renders them as bare abstractions and therefore as replaceable and expendable:

> Are we to attribute to the divine Friend and Lover of men a levity of attitude which we find offensively untrue of our ordinary human fidelities? Are we to liken Him to a military commander, who is content if fresh drafts are forthcoming to fill his depleted battalions? To the military system, men are only so much human material, so many numerable units; but a chance encounter with one of the men in the flesh, one touch of human-heartedness, is sufficient to dissolve the abstraction which so regards them.[103]

He goes on to add that personal immortality, although "too good *not* to be true,"[104] is not to be founded upon any claims about the intrinsic nature of human beings. Immortality is not "an inherent possession of every human soul, or a talismanic gift conferred indiscriminately on every being born in human shape."[105] Immortality is not ours by nature, something freely granted; nor is it ours by right, something we deserve or is owed to us.[106] Rather, it is "a matter of achievement";[107] genuine personality or selfhood "is emphatically something that must be won before there can be any question of its conservation,"[108] which implies that the dissolution of the individual self or mind is possible after all (as Pringle-Pattison himself concedes).[109]

Despite accepting personal survival, Pringle-Pattison does not think that we ought to adopt an otherworldly (mystic, ascetic) attitude toward death and the afterlife.[110] This attitude has frequently been associated with Plato's *Phaedo*, where the soul, upon physical death, escapes the prison-house of the body and achieves endless life. For Pringle-Pattison, the negative attitude adopted by Plato to the present life and its concerns, and the allied dualism between the present and the afterlife, cannot be justified. Pringle-Pattison detects in Spinoza a more positive and plausible perspective on death: "There is nothing on which the free man lets his thoughts dwell less than on death," Spinoza is quoted as saying; and Spinoza immediately adds, against Plato, that "the free man's wisdom is not a meditation of death but of life."[111] Physical death, on this view, is not an evil that threatens to undermine the value of life—in fact, death "doesn't count,"[112] it "cannot touch the life of the spirit,"[113] and so it's not worth bothering about. What counts is *memento vivere* (Goethe's inversion of Plato), remembering to live a good and full life, in the manner of fellow idealist Richard Lewis Nettleship, whose memorial plaque in Balliol College reads:

> He loved great things and thought little of himself: desiring nei-ther fame nor influence, he won the devotion of men and was a power in their lives: and seeking no disciples, he taught to many the greatness of the world and of man's mind.[114]

3.5.3

If we revert to the existentialist perspective, the foregoing debate between Pringle-Pattison and Bosanquet might be seen in a new light. If, in particular, the existentialist perspective on death and fini-tude is brought into play, it becomes evident that, although Pringle-Pattison's personal idealism makes more room for personality and allied notions (such as individual autonomy) than does the absolute idealism of Bosanquet, both forms of idealism fall foul of the existen-tialist imperative to genuinely face up to mortality and, in this way, to live 'authentically.'

The prominence of death in existentialism is well known, even appearing to some critics as a morbid obsession. In a reversal of centuries-old Platonic dualism—where death is defined as the sepa-ration of two distinct entities: body and soul, with the latter but not the former indestructible by nature—existentialist writers and think-ers took the finality of death as crushing any hope for immortality. Death, therefore, looms large in existentialism, as its implications are considered profound, in both positive and negative ways, yet these are regularly overlooked. For the existentialist, as John Macquarrie has observed, "death is not simply the termination of life, not just an event that comes along at the end of the story, but itself enters very much into the story."[115] And it enters the story in different ways, so that for some (temporal) finitude is regarded a precondition for freedom and individuality. As Sartre expresses the point:

> There is freedom if there is a choice among possibles. And an irremediable choice. In other words, if it is understood that all the possibles *will not be realized*. If a being were endowed with a temporal infinity, he could realize every possible, he would therefore be nothing more than the development in an infinite and necessary series of every possible, therefore he would disappear as an individuality (the realization of these possibles to the exclusion of all the rest) and as freedom (the dangerous and irremediable choice of some possibles).[116]

Heidegger, similarly, links Dasein to death: "Only in dying can I to some extent say absolutely, 'I am,'" he writes.[117] The being of Dasein is structured as being-toward-death (*Sein zum Tode*), with death understood not so much in biological terms (what Heidegger calls 'demise'), but in an existential sense as the "possibility of the absolute impossibility of Dasein."[118] The typical, inauthentic comportment toward this possibility is one of evasion and concealment, distancing oneself from it by relegating it to an indeterminate future where it poses no real threat: "One dies too, sometime," *das Man* admits, "but not right away."[119] The path, indeed the sole path, to overcoming the sway of this orientation, and thus achieving authenticity, can be found in the full and honest recognition of death as constitutive of Dasein. But this is no easy path, as it can be cleared only through the unsettling experience of anxiety or dread (*Angst*) in being "wrenched away from the 'they'"[120] and thrown back onto one's own resources as one comes to terms with one's finitude and mortality. What this experience reveals is the ultimate contingency of our commitments, which are not rooted (as the British idealists suppose) in some transcendent principle or metaphysical ground (the Absolute, God), but which lack any such foundations: this is the nullity at the heart of things disclosed by anxiety. This lack, thinks Heidegger, may provoke a crisis, indicating to Dasein the fragile nature of all its possibilities, while also undoing Dasein's relations with others as it becomes frozen by the complete insignificance of the world.[121] At the same time, however, this presents an opportunity to recover one's self from immersion in the distractions of the They, to find one's true self and freedom, not by fleeing from death but by resolutely facing up to it as the possibility of being that is most one's own. As Stephen Mulhall nicely puts it,

> Dasein thereby comes to see that its life is something for which it is responsible, that it is its own to live (or to disown)—that its existence makes a claim on it that is essentially non-relational, not something to be sloughed off on to Others.[122]

To delve deeper into the existentialist view of death, I wish to return to Camus, for whom the pressing finality of death is a major theme across his literary and philosophical works. I will concentrate, however, on his brilliant first novel, *L'Étranger*[123] (published in 1942, though written over 1937–40), where the awareness of death is closely connected to the experience of absurdity, and where the proposed response to both is a conscious revolt that infuses life with authenticity and vitality (as opposed to defeatist resignation or suicide).

It might be worth beginning with a word about Camus' relationship to religion and religious views about the afterlife, which has often been misunderstood. Like many of his fellow French existentialists, Camus' starting-point was Nietzsche's proclamation that 'God is dead.' But this did not mean Camus was an atheist, at least in any straightforward sense. Camus, constantly defined and compelled to define himself as an atheist, was asked at one point by an interviewer to explain his comment: "Secret of my universe: imagine God without the immortality of the soul." By way of explanation, Camus responded: "I have a sense of the sacred and I don't believe in a future life, that's all."[124]

To see what exactly this rejection of the afterlife amounts to in Camus' thought, it might be helpful to look to Meursault, the protagonist of *L'Étranger*, portrayed there as an alienated outsider, but intriguingly described by Camus as "the only Christ we deserve" in his preface to the American edition.[125] Meursault, a young and unambitious office worker in French colonial Algiers, leads a content and unexceptional life but also one that is curiously distant and detached, taking as he does an unsentimental and ironic attitude toward the typical bourgeois values of love, marriage, and work. Everything changes, however, when he kills an unnamed Arab on a beach, seemingly accidentally or impulsively: although the Arab had drawn a knife on him, no coherent explanation is given as to why Meursault shot him (rather than avoiding the confrontation), or why he went on to fire four extra shots. If anything, the impression given is of Meursault as a passive victim of the oppressive summer heat: "the trigger gave," the narrative runs.[126] In line with this, his only defence at the trial that follows is "because of the sun,"[127] but the jury finds him guilty and he is promptly sentenced to death.

While awaiting execution, a chaplain makes an unannounced visit, Meursault having previously declined to see him no less than three times. In their initial exchange Meursault is indifferent and dismissive, telling the chaplain that "I'd very little time left, and I wasn't going to waste it on God."[128] He also admits to the chaplain that "I didn't believe in God"[129] and that he "didn't want to be helped" by God.[130] When the discussion turns to death and his looming execution, Meursault rejects any hope of an afterlife, upholding instead the view that "when you die you die outright, and nothing remains."[131] He similarly refuses the chaplain's attempt to have him concede some consciousness of guilt or sinfulness, or even some sense of divinity (to recognize "a divine face" in the prison walls).[132] And even though Meursault does acknowledge the desire at least to survive death, this, he replies, "had no more importance than wishing to be rich, or to swim very fast, or to have a better-shaped mouth."[133] Very quickly, however, Meursault's attitude turns from indifference to irritation and thence to raging hostility. The trigger comes in the form of the question of solidarity: Meursault refuses to address the priest as 'Father,' telling him that "he wasn't my father; quite the contrary, he was on the others' side."[134] In response, the priest places his hand on Meursault's shoulder and patronizingly tells him: "No, no, my son. I'm on *your* side, though you don't realize it—because your heart is hardened. But I shall pray for you."[135] At this, Meursault loses his cool and explodes. He grabs the priest by the collar of his cassock and starts insulting him and yelling at him. Meursault tells him that he doesn't want his prayers, that "none of his certainties was worth one strand of a woman's hair,"[136] and—most importantly for our purposes—that all he (Meursault) could be sure of was "my present life and the death that was coming. That, no doubt, was all I had; but at least that certainty was something I could get my teeth into—just as it had got its teeth into me."[137]

In this reverie of rage, Meursault realizes that "nothing, nothing had the least importance, and I knew quite well why"[138]—the reason why, he goes on to explain, lying in the fact that all are "condemned to die." This marks a turning-point for Meursault, one expressed with memorable pathos:

> From the dark horizon of my future a sort of slow, persistent breeze had been blowing toward me, all my life long, from the years that

were to come. And on its way that breeze had leveled out all the ideas that people tried to foist on me in the equally unreal years I then was living through. What difference could they make to me, the deaths of others, or a mother's love, or his God; or the way a man decides to live, the fate he thinks he chooses, since one and the same fate was bound to 'choose' not only me but thousands of millions of privileged people who, like him, called themselves my brothers. Surely, surely he must see that? Every man alive was privileged; there was only one class of men, the privileged class. All alike would be condemned to die one day.[139]

The prison guards soon rush in to the chaplain's rescue, releasing him from Meursault's grip. With the chaplain gone and alone once more in his cell, Meursault falls asleep from exhaustion. On awaking before daybreak, his newfound awareness continues, first with a fresh appreciation for the sounds and smells of the summer night. Then, "for the first time in many months,"[140] he thought of his recently deceased mother who, he surmises, attained towards the end of her life a new sense of freedom, making her "ready to start life all over again."[141] He therefore concludes that "no one, no one in the world had any right to weep for her."[142] And by implication no one should weep for him either, for like his mother he now felt ready for a new start:

> It was as if that great rush of anger had washed me clean, emptied me of hope, and, gazing up at the dark sky spangled with its signs and stars, for the first time, the first, I laid my heart open to the benign indifference of the universe. To feel it so like myself, indeed, so brotherly, made me realize that I'd been happy, and that I was happy still.[143]

This was Meursault's achievement of 'tragic consciousness.' Whereas earlier he lived nonchalantly, as a sensory rather than a reflective being, "absorbed in the present moment, or the immediate future," as he at one point admits,[144] he begins to come to consciousness after the shooting and especially while awaiting execution. What he specifically begins to recognize is his terrible fate (the finality of death) and the consequent absurdity of existence, which negates 'cosmic' or ultimate meaning: nothing really matters, one act is as good or bad as any other. But this unflinching consciousness of the tragic truth does not negate meaning altogether. Rather, and somewhat paradoxically, the very thing—death—that robs life of objective worth is also what makes our choices urgent and momentous, and our lives immeasurably precious, at least on a personal and existential level. Meursault begins to appreciate the value of life only when it is in danger of being lost, but it is this that affords him a new lease on life, awakening an inner peace and freedom in the recognition of what he calls "the benign indifference of the universe."[145] As Camus said of Sisyphus in a contemporaneous work, one must imagine Meursault happy.[146]

Returning to Camus' comments in his preface to the novel's American edition, he pictures Meursault there as a model of authenticity, arguing that his very authenticity is what landed him in trouble. Consider, for example, Camus' concise summary of the novel: "In our society a man who does not weep at his mother's funeral runs the risk of being sentenced to death."[147] Meursault is condemned less for shooting an Arab than for his failure to exhibit conventionally expected emotions, his failure to "play the game," as Camus says.[148] And Meursault doesn't play the game, Camus explains, in the sense that "he refuses to lie."[149] His refusal to participate in the customary dissembling practices by which absurdity is kept at bay is precisely what makes him, in the eyes of society, an outsider, and a threatening one at that. The afterlife, of course, is one of the 'lies' which Meursault refuses to swallow, choosing instead to remain true to his experience of the "slow, persistent breeze...blowing toward me, all my life long." Camus therefore asks us to see Meursault, not as the shallow or even inhumane character he is sometimes interpreted as being,[150] but as someone animated by "a passion for the absolute and for truth," someone prepared, Christ-like, "to die for the truth"—the truth that we will all die, unlike Christ, without the possibility of resurrection.[151]

Notes

1 Parts of this chapter draw upon my paper, "Life and Finite Individuality: Revisiting a debate in British Idealism," published in Simon Kittle and Georg Gasser (eds), *The Divine Nature: Personal and A-Personal Perspectives* (New York: Routledge, 2022), pp.42–61. I gratefully acknowledge the permission of the publisher to make use of this material.

2 More recently (on April 19, 2019), Slavoj Žižek and Jordan Peterson met before a sold-out audience in Toronto, Canada to debate 'Happiness: Capitalism vs Marxism.' One wonders what the philosophical merits are of such debates, which often resemble bloodsports held before jeering and cheering crowds, or evangelical church gatherings aimed at preaching to the faithful and, possibly, converting the rest (think only of William Lane Craig's so-called 'debates' on the existence of God and other issues in philosophy of religion).

3 The debate was published in the *Proceedings of the Aristotelian Society, 18* (1917–18), 479–581, with contributions by Bernard Bosanquet,

A. S. Pringle-Pattison, G. F. Stout, and R. B. Haldane. Subsequent references to this will be abbreviated as 'Aristotelian Society debate.'

4 Andrew Seth had 'Pringle-Pattison' added to his name in 1898 in order to fulfil the conditions of accepting a bequest.

5 David Burrell, *Faith and Freedom: An Interfaith Perspective* (Oxford: Blackwell, 2004), p.220.

6 Brian Davies, "Simplicity," in Charles Taliaferro and Chad Meister (eds), *The Cambridge Companion to Christian Philosophical Theology* (Cambridge: Cambridge University Press, 2010), p.31.

7 Ibid., pp.33–4.

8 Ibid., p.34.

9 Ibid., p.36, emphases in original.

10 See Charles Hartshorne, *The Zero Fallacy and Other Essays in Neoclassical Philosophy*, ed. Mohammad Valady (Chicago, IL: Open Court, 1997), pp.6, 39.

11 Alfred North Whitehead, *Process and Reality: An Essay in Cosmology*, corrected edn, ed. David Ray Griffin and Donald W. Sherburne (New York: The Free Press, 1985, originally published 1929), p.351.

12 Charles Hartshorne, *The Divine Relativity: A Social Conception of God* (New Haven, CT: Yale University Press, 1948), p.54.

13 See Boethius, *The Consolation of Philosophy*, book V, where he differentiates God's eternity from the kind of everlasting temporal duration ascribed by some ancients to the world: "For it is one thing to progress like the world in Plato's theory through everlasting life, and another thing to have embraced the whole of everlasting life in one simultaneous present" (trans. V. E. Watts, London: Penguin, 1969, p.164).

14 Robert C. Coburn, "Professor Malcolm on God," *Australasian Journal of Philosophy, 41* (1963), 155. In a similar vein, Coburn goes on to argue (on pp.155–6) that a timeless being could not know everything which (logically) can be known. It is perhaps possible here to detect the influence of process theology upon Coburn, who studied under Hartshorne at the University of Chicago.

15 Bosanquet states: "we mean [by 'individuality'] that which must stand; that which has nothing without to set against it, and which is pure self-maintenance within" (*Principle of Individuality and Value*, London: Macmillan, 1912, p.68).

16 W. J. Mander, "In Defence of the Eternal Consciousness," in Maria Dimova-Cookson and W. J. Mander (eds), *T. H. Green: Ethics, Metaphysics, and Political Philosophy* (Oxford: Clarendon Press, 2006), p.190, emphases in original.

17 Olive Anderson, "The Feminism of T. H. Green: A Late-Victorian Success Story?" *History of Political Thought, 12* (1991), 685.

18 Bosanquet says that the conception of an 'infinite being' "appears to be formed by denying every predicate which we attach to personality" ("On the True Conception of Another World," in *Essays and Addresses*, 2nd edn (London: Swan Sonnenschein, 1891), p.99). Elsewhere he writes that "the God of religion…is an appearance of reality, as distinct from being the whole and ultimate reality; a rank which religion cannot consistently claim for the supreme being as it must conceive him" (*The Value and Destiny of the Individual* (London: Macmillan, 1923), pp.255–6). Cf. Bradley's

statement: "If you identify the Absolute with God, that is not the God of religion" (*Appearance and Reality*, 2nd edn, 9th impression (Oxford: Clarendon Press, 1930), p.395).

19 For Green, this unity is secured by relations, but for Bosanquet and Bradley, relations are thought to have the opposite effect, of sundering that which was whole, and so they regard ultimate reality as wholly non-relational (or 'supra-relational': see Bradley, *Appearance and Reality*, 2nd edn, p.494). Despite this effect had by relations, Bosanquet upholds "the general indivisible spirit of things" ("Unvisited Tombs," *Some Suggestions in Ethics* (London: Macmillan, 1919), p.85).

20 Bosanquet, *Principle of Individuality and Value*, p.255.

21 Ibid., p.372.

22 Bosanquet, Aristotelian Society debate, p.497. See also *Principle of Individuality and Value*, p.221.

23 Bosanquet, "On 'Doubting the Reality of Evil,'" in *Some Suggestions in Ethics*, p.102.

24 Bosanquet, Aristotelian Society debate, p.499.

25 As Bosanquet was aware, Keats thought of this scheme as "a grander system of salvation than the Christian religion" (*Value and Destiny of the Individual*, p.65).

26 Bosanquet, *Principle of Individuality and Value*, pp.270–1.

27 Bosanquet at this point makes reference to Bradley's *Appearance and Reality*, 2nd edn, p.529 (or pp.468–9 in the first edition), where Bradley argues that the Absolute does not consist in souls or selves.

28 Bosanquet, *Principle of Individuality and Value*, p.250, emphasis mine.

29 Another Advaitan analogy, again pointing to this notion of absorption, likens Brahman to Space and individual selves to the space within jars. When the jars are destroyed, the space in the jars merges back into Space. Enlightenment (*moksha*) breaks open the jars, and individual identity is finally absorbed into pure, undifferentiated Brahman. To quote Shankara (early eighth century, traditionally 788–820 CE), the most prominent member of the Advaita tradition: "As the space in a jar in universal space, so the Self is to be merged without division in the Self supreme" (*Crest-Jewel of Wisdom*, verse 288).

30 David Hume, *A Treatise of Human Nature*, ed. Ernest C. Mossner (London: Penguin, 1984, originally published 1739–40), p.301.

31 But note Christopher Gowans' view (in *Philosophy of the Buddha*, London: Routledge, 2003, ch. 6) that, in Buddhism, it is not merely the case that substance-selves have no reality (because there are no substances, in accord with the doctrine of 'emptiness'), but even process-selves are not ultimately real—the reality they have is only a 'dependent reality' (where something has dependent reality if its reality directly depends on mental states).

32 This gives us Bosanquet's holistic theory of judgement: instead of ascribing predicates to finite things (as we normally do), all predicates are referred to reality as a whole. Thus, instead of affirming 'S is P' (e.g., Jones is tall), we attribute the S–P connection to Reality and say: *Reality is such that at or in S it is P* (e.g., Reality is such that at or in Jones it is tall). (Aristotelian Society debate, p.484).

33 Andrew Seth, *Hegelianism and Personality*, 2nd edn (Edinburgh: William Blackwood and Sons, 1893), p.226.

34 Ibid., p.227, emphasis in original.
35 Ibid., p.228.
36 Seth Pringle-Pattison, *The Idea of God in the Light of Recent Philosophy*, 2nd edn (New York: Oxford University Press, 1920), p.256.
37 Ibid., pp.257–8.
38 Ibid., p.258.
39 I owe this to W. J. Mander, *British Idealism: A History* (Oxford: Oxford University Press, 2011), p.189.
40 Pringle-Pattison, *The Idea of God*, pp.261–2.
41 Ibid., p.264.
42 Ibid., p.264.
43 Ibid., p.266; see also p.278. Note also the criticism made of Bosanquet's soul-making theory by another personal idealist, Clement C. J. Webb, in "Bernard Bosanquet's Philosophy of Religion," *The Hibbert Journal* (1923), 89–90.
44 Pringle-Pattison, *The Idea of God*, p.266.
45 Ibid., p.267.
46 Ibid., p.269.
47 Ibid., p.272.
48 For Pringle-Pattison's attempt to link Bosanquet's conception of the individual to Spinoza's account of substance, see the Aristotelian Society debate, p.509.
49 Pringle-Pattison, *The Idea of God*, p.272; Aristotelian Society debate, p.510.
50 Pringle-Pattison, Aristotelian Society debate, p.510.
51 Pringle-Pattison, *The Idea of God*, p.282.
52 Ibid., pp.273–5.
53 Ibid., p.277.
54 Bradley puts forward this doctrine in *Ethical Studies* (first published in 1876) but also lists a series of "very serious objections" to it. In the process, he acknowledges duties or activities (e.g., science, art) that might be pursued as ends in themselves without appeal to any social organism. See F. H. Bradley, *Ethical Studies*, 2nd edn (London: Oxford University Press, 1962), pp.202–5.
55 Hegel contrasted this form of morality with *Moralität*, an individualist ethic which he associated with Kant and with such notions as conscience, inner will and intention.
56 Jean-Paul Sartre, *Existentialism and Humanism*, trans. Philip Mairet (London: Methuen and Co., 1948), p.41. Sartre also hints at this performative aspect of selfhood in *The Transcendence of the Ego: An Existentialist Theory of Consciousness*, trans. Forrest Williams and Robert Kirkpatrick (New York: Hill and Wang, 1960), p.94. This was Sartre's first major work (published in 1936–37), where he argues against the notion of the 'transcendental ego' that was central to German idealism and Husserlian phenomenology.
57 Jean-Paul Sartre, *'No Exit' and Three Other Plays* (New York: Vintage, 1989), p.45.
58 As Thomas Anderson, relying upon Sartre's *Cahiers pour une morale*, has pointed out, the 'hell' of other people was not seen by Sartre as "an inevitable ontological condition, nor a necessary result of history, but

a free human decision," and one that can be set right through 'conversion' ("Sartre's Early Ethics and the Ontology of *Being and Nothingness*," in Charles Guignon (ed.), *The Existentialists: Critical Essays on Kierkegaard, Nietzsche, Heidegger, and Sartre*, Lanham, MD: Rowman and Littlefield Publishers, 2004, p.146).

59 Thomas R. Flynn, "Sartre," in Simon Critchley and William R. Schroeder (eds), *A Companion to Continental Philosophy* (Malden, MA: Blackwell, 1999), p.261.

60 Sartre, *Between Existentialism and Marxism*, trans. John Matthews (London: NLB, 1974), p.35.

61 Although the above critique of the Absolute Idealist view of the self relies heavily on Sartre's version of existentialism, a similar critique can be developed from the works of other existentialists. Nietzsche, for example, is well known for his rejection of disciples and his encouragement of independence from the confining conventions of society, religion, and morality. In an early work, *Untimely Meditations* (1873–76), he begins to use the expression 'authentic human being' as a way of contrasting genuine individuality from the machine-like existence demanded by contemporary culture. Similarly in *Daybreak* (1881), which he later (in *Ecce Homo*, 1888) called his "crusade against morality," the morality of modernity is characterized in terms of the individual denying itself and adapting to the whole, thereby cancelling its true self and developing a 'phantom ego' formed by the opinions of others:

> as a consequence they all of them dwell in a fog of impersonal, semi-personal opinions, and arbitrary, as it were poetical evaluations, the one for ever in the head of someone else, and the head of this someone else again in the heads of others: a strange world of phantasms—which at the same time knows how to put on so sober an appearance!
> (*Daybreak: Thoughts on the Prejudices of Morality*, trans. R. J. Hollingdale, ed. Maudemarie Clark and Brian Leiter, Cambridge: Cambridge University Press, 1997, §105, p. 61)

Note also Nietzsche's conceptions of the 'free spirit' and the 'will to power,' exemplified in those with the strength and courage to think for themselves, to free themselves from traditional constraints, and to create and live by their own values as sovereign individuals. See, for example, *The Gay Science* §§335, 347; and *Beyond Good and Evil*, part two, esp. §§41–44. This is not to overlook Nietzsche's antipathy toward extreme individualism, encapsulated in the figure of Socrates and ushering an age of decadence in Greek culture—see especially "The Problem of Socrates" in *The Twilight of the Idols*. Interestingly, one of the few British engagements with Nietzsche before the Great War came from Pringle-Pattison, who wrote two articles on Nietzsche's life and thought in 1897–98. These were collected in Pringle-Pattison's *Man's Place in the Cosmos and Other Essays*, 2nd edn (Edinburgh: William Blackwood and Sons, 1902), pp.254–319. It's worth noting Pringle-Pattison's comment that Nietzsche "preaches a doctrine of the most intense individualism," and that, "in…loosening the individual from his social and political surroundings, Nietzsche pursues his individualism to the verge of anarchism" (p.304).

Consider, also, Heidegger's negative stance toward *das Man*, the anonymous 'they' and their 'idle talk' (*Gerede*), always posing a threat to Dasein, even as sociality is constitutive of Dasein, which is thoroughly enmeshed and entangled in the world. Nonetheless Dasein, alone of all entities, *exists* or has *existence* in the etymological sense of *ek-sistence*—i.e., as a standing out, so that only Dasein can stand back or 'out' from its own occurrence in the world and make up its own mind, be true to its own self, and thus achieve authenticity (*Eigentlichkeit*).

Consider, finally, Kierkegaard's valorization of 'the single individual' against Hegel's prioritization of the social or universal:

> Faith is precisely the paradox that the single individual as the single individual is higher than the universal, is justified before it, not as inferior to it but as superior—but in such a way...that the single individual as the single individual stands in an absolute relation to the absolute.
>
> (*Fear and Trembling; Repetition*, ed. and trans. Howard V. Hong and Edna H. Hong, Princeton, NJ: Princeton University Press, 1983, pp.55–6)

Hegel, according to Kierkegaard, renders existential questions and pursuits redundant. In Hegel's system, there is no need to ask or choose how to live—the path is already laid out (objectively) in advance. As Kierkegaard jests, a man who wonders whether he is truly a Christian might receive the following reply from his wife if she were a Hegelian:

> Hubby, darling, where did you ever pick up such a notion? How can you not be a Christian? You are Danish, aren't you? Doesn't the geography book say that the predominant religion in Denmark is Lutheran-Christian? You aren't a Jew, are you, or a Mohammedan? What else would you be, then?
>
> (*Concluding Unscientific Postscript to 'Philosophical Fragments,'* p.50)

For Kierkegaard, faith is far from easy, but "a task for a whole lifetime" (*Fear and Trembling*, p.7). One cannot fall back on pre-established givens or certainties (e.g., those of one's community), but must work at fashioning one's own identity. This, however, is the highest task of all, requiring the cultivation of an 'inward deepening,' relating to (say) the message of Christianity with a personal, passionate interest, not speculatively or dispassionately, thus replacing abstraction with 'appropriation'—which means risk, isolation and above all suffering greatly. Kierkegaard repeatedly insists that *suffering* is essential to the Christian life, and that this insight had been forgotten (or obscured, suppressed, even rejected) in the Christianity of his age, being replaced instead by a 'thin' and 'soft' variety of Christian practice. These ideas are littered throughout his journals: see Kierkegaard, *Papers and Journals: A Selection*, trans. Alastair Hannay (London: Penguin, 1996), pp.568, 577, 614, 631, 633, 644–5, 648. Note also his words from his death-bed: "Tell them my life is a big, and to others unknown and incomprehensible, suffering" (p.653).

62 Bosanquet, "Unvisited Tombs," pp.84–5.

63 Ibid. p.85. In previous sections of the essay, Bosanquet placed much emphasis on the unity of the world, and in particular the unity of humanity with the external or natural world.

64 Ibid., pp.85–6.

65 Ibid., p.86.

66 Ibid., p.87. Cf. John Caird's sermon, "Corporate Immortality," in his *University Sermons Preached before the University of Glasgow 1873–1898* (Glasgow: James MacLehose and Sons, 1898), pp.176–95. Caird there defends a form of immortality much like Bosanquet's in not requiring individual survival and in not conceiving of heaven as a timeless, otherworldly state or region. Caird exhorts his audience:

> You can think and desire and work for more than the petty interests of your brief individual life, because you *are* more and greater than the individual, because it is possible for you to share in a universal and undying life, with the future of which your most boundless aspirations are not incompatible.
>
> (p.189, emphasis in original)

67 Bosanquet, *Value and Destiny of the Individual*, p.4. 'Completeness,' in Bosanquet's lexicon, designates full concreteness, the highest level of being or reality. For him, therefore, the opposite of completeness is *abstraction*, where some aspect of an individual's being is ignored or partitioned off.

68 Bosanquet, Aristotelian Society debate, pp.500–1.

69 See Bosanquet, "The Reality of the General Will," in Bosanquet (ed.), *Aspects of the Social Problem* (London: Macmillan and Co., 1895), pp.319–32; and Bosanquet's "Reply" in H. Wildon Carr (ed.), *Life and Infinite Individuality* (London: Williams and Norgate, 1918), p.185.

70 Bosanquet, *Principle of Individuality and Value*, p.37.

71 Ibid., p.38.

72 Avital Simhony, "'To Set Free the Idea of the Self': Bosanquet's Relational Individual," in W. J. Mander and Stamatoula Panagakou (eds), *British Idealism and the Concept of the Self* (London: Palgrave Macmillan, 2016), pp.213–15.

73 The notion of 'strong relationality' is one that Simhony borrows from the psychologist, Brent D. Slife, who espouses a radical relational approach to psychotherapy.

74 Bosanquet, Aristotelian Society debate, p.492.

75 Ibid., p.506. Bosanquet detects a similar view in his former teacher, T.H. Green. Although Green insisted on the conservation of personality, this did not prevent him (according to Bosanquet) from seeing that there might be other, more valuable and more permanent, ways of being than as a finite consciousness. Consider, for example, the following passage, where Bosanquet reads Green as holding that what ultimately survives, once the self achieves full realization, is not the nominal or personal self (with which we are familiar now), but an expanded self (which is more, not less, than personal):

> The necessity insisted on throughout that the goal of development shall be nothing short of a personal self-consciousness, does not, I

think, signify for the author [i.e. Green] in the last resort an emphasis on the conscious continuance of you or me, with unbroken identity, keeping us one with an earthly past, within or into the ultimate
being. In the last resort I believe that it means simply and solely this:
that the contents, the interests, the qualitative experience and focus-
sing of externality, which are our best—i.e. our whole in its fullest adjustment—and the centre of our being, for which so far as we
understand ourselves we would readily sacrifice our nominal self—
that all these things find their full development in the ultimate being,
and in a form of experience not lower, but higher than what we call
personality. In a word, then, what is held essential is not primarily
that the goal of development should be *our* personality, but that it
shall be *a* personality; and the doctrine has nothing against its being
more than a personality, so long as in it all that constituted ourself
can have fuller justice done to it than in our given self it ever could
have. We, both our form—I mean, our peculiarly qualified individual
self-consciousness—and our content—I mean, our interests and
experiences—are thus real and eternal in the ultimate being.

(*Value and Destiny of the Individual*, pp.281–2, emphases in original)

76 Bosanquet, *Value and Destiny of the Individual*, p.68.
77 Ibid, p.261.
78 Ibid.
79 Andrew Seth, *Hegelianism and Personality*, pp.235–6.
80 Ibid., p.236.
81 Ibid., p.237.
82 Ibid., p.238.
83 Ibid., p.239.
84 Ibid., p.240.
85 Pringle-Pattison, *The Idea of God*, p.267.
86 Pringle-Pattison, Aristotelian Society debate, p.524, emphasis in original; cf. p.511.
87 Ibid., p.524.
88 Ibid., p.525, emphasis in original.
89 Ibid., p.526.
90 Ibid., p.517. See also p.523, where he says: "My position…is that belief in
the relative independence of human personalities and belief in the existence of God as a living Being are bound up together."
91 Pringle-Pattison, *The Idea of God*, pp.407–9.
92 Ibid., pp.409–11.
93 On this criticism, see Mander, *British Idealism*, p.411, who reads
Pringle-Pattison as thinking of divine transcendence in axiological, not
ontological, terms.
94 Pringle-Pattison, *The Idea of God*, p.411.
95 Ibid., p.390. But Pringle-Pattison immediately qualifies this to emphasize
that the personality of God is not be understood along the lines of a finite
consciousness: "… an experience not limited to the intermittent and fragmentary glimpses of this and the other finite consciousness, but resuming
the whole life of the world in a fashion which is necessarily incomprehensible save by the Absolute itself" (p. 390).

96 Pringle-Pattison similarly contends, *contra* Bosanquet, that accepting the relational nature of the finite self need not lead to the dissolution of the self:

> But because a mind cannot be extracted and exhibited as a self-contained whole apart from 'the moral and spiritual structure' in which it is rooted, it does not follow that the mind or self is simply a punctual centre in which a system of moral and social relations reflects itself into unity as rays of light are concentrated in a focus.
>
> (Aristotelian Society debate, pp.517–18)

97 Pringle-Pattison, *The Idea of Immortality* (Oxford: Clarendon Press, 1922), p.157. See also Pringle-Pattison's remarks at pp.526–7 of the Aristotelian Society debate, where he charges Bosanquet as holding (or coming close to holding) a "pagan, egoistic or self-centred view of the Absolute," which Pringle-Pattison contrasts with a Christian conception of the divine nature as loving and other-centred, in which case "the otherness must be real and not only apparent."

98 Pringle-Pattison, *The Idea of Immortality*, p.160.

99 Ibid.

100 Pringle-Pattison, *The Idea of God*, p.289.

101 Pringle-Pattison, *The Idea of Immortality*, p.164.

102 Ibid., p.167. Pringle-Pattison also makes this criticism in the Aristotelian Society debate, pp.525–6. But see Mander, *British Idealism*, p.389, who draws upon the analogy of a multinational corporation and its sub-companies to argue that the merging of parts need not result in the destruction of the original identities of the parts.

103 Pringle-Pattison, *The Idea of Immortality*, p.191. The passage is taken verbatim from Pringle-Pattison's contribution to the Aristotelian Society debate, p.528.

104 Pringle-Pattison, *The Idea of Immortality*, p.193, emphasis in original (Pringle-Pattison notes that this saying is attributed by Henry Jones to Emerson). In defense of this view, Pringle-Pattison states that "the permanent ideals which have lighted mankind on its way must be taken as our best clue to the inmost nature of the real" (p.195).

105 Ibid., p.195; cf. Aristotelian Society debate, p.514.

106 Pringle-Pattison, Aristotelian Society debate, p.516.

107 Ibid., p.514; cf. p.529.

108 Pringle-Pattison, *The Idea of Immortality*, p.196.

109 See Pringle-Pattison, Aristotelian Society debate, p.529.

110 Pringle-Pattison, *The Idea of Immortality*, pp.206–8.

111 Ibid., p.207. Pringle-Pattison is quoting from Spinoza's *Ethics* IV.67.

112 Pringle-Pattison, *The Idea of Immortality*, p.207.

113 Ibid., p.208.

114 Quoted in Pringle-Pattison, *The Idea of Immortality*, p.208.

115 Macquarrie, *Existentialism* (Harmondsworth: Penguin, 1973), p.151.

116 Sartre, *Notebooks for an Ethics*, trans. David Pellauer (Chicago, IL: The University of Chicago Press, 1992), p.326, emphasis in original. Although posthumously published, this work was written in 1947–48 to fulfill the promise of an 'ethics of authenticity' made in his masterwork, *Being and Nothingness* (1943). Sartre's thinking here is reminiscent of Bernard

Williams' argument that immortality would be a grave misfortune as it
would deprive people of the 'categorical desires' with which they identify
and which make life meaningful. See Bernard Williams, "The Makropulos Case: Reflections on the Tedium of Immortality," in *Problems of the
Self* (Cambridge: Cambridge University Press, 1973), pp.82–100.

117 Heidegger, *History of the Concept of Time: Prolegomena*, trans. Theodore
Kisiel (Bloomington: Indiana University Press, 1992), p.318.

118 Heidegger, *Being and Time*, trans. John Macquarrie and Edward Robin-
son (Malden, MA: Blackwell Publishing, 1962), §50, p.294. A good sum-
mary of Heidegger's existential understanding of death is provided by
William Blattner, "Heidegger: The Existential Analytic of Dasein," in
Crowell (ed.), *The Cambridge Companion to Existentialism* (Cambridge:
Cambridge University Press, 2012), pp.168–9.

119 Heidegger, *Being and Time*, §52, p.299.

120 Ibid., §53, p.307.

121 Ibid., §40, p.231.

122 Stephen Mulhall, *Routledge Philosophy Guidebook to Heidegger and
'Being and Time,'* 2nd edn (London: Routledge, 2005), p.129.

123 Translated as *The Stranger* in the US, and *The Outsider* in the UK.

124 From a 1959 interview, in Camus, *Lyrical and Critical Essays*, p.364.
Note also Camus' comment: "I hear people speak of my atheism. Yet the
words say nothing to me: for me they have no meaning. I do not believe
in God *and* I am not an atheist" (*Notebooks: 1951–1959*, trans. Ryan
Bloom, Chicago, IL: Ivan R. Dee, 2008, p.112, emphasis in the original).
T. S. Eliot's assessment of Tennyson's poem *In Memoriam* might provide
a further clue as to the nature of Camus' relation to religion: "It is not
religious because of the quality of its faith, but because of the quality of
its doubt. Its faith is a poor thing, but its doubt is a very intense experience. *In Memoriam* is a poem of despair, but of despair of a religious
kind" (*Selected Prose of T. S. Eliot*, ed. Frank Kermode, New York:
Harcourt Brace Jovanovich, 1975, p.245).

125 In Camus, *Lyrical and Critical Essays*, p.337.

126 Camus, *The Stranger*, trans. Stuart Gilbert (New York: Alfred A. Knopf,
1974), p.76.

127 Ibid., p.130.

128 Ibid., p.150.

129 Ibid., p.145.

130 Ibid., p.146.

131 Ibid., p.147.

132 Ibid., p.149.

133 Ibid., p.150.

134 Ibid.

135 Ibid., pp.150–1, emphasis in original.

136 Ibid., p.151.

137 Ibid.

138 Ibid., p.152.

139 Ibid.

140 Ibid., p.153.

141 Ibid., p.154. Meursault is here referring to the close relationship his mother
formed at the nursing home with fellow resident, Thomas Pérez (see p.15).

142 Ibid., p.154.
143 Ibid.
144 Ibid., p.127.
145 As Camus expresses the point in *The Myth of Sisyphus*:

> It was previously a question of finding out whether or not life had to have a meaning to be lived. It now becomes clear on the contrary that it will be lived all the better if it has no meaning.
>
> (p.53)

146 Or as Camus was to say in a later essay ("Return to Tipasa," 1952), "In the middle of winter, I at last discovered that there was in me an invincible summer" (in *The Myth of Sisyphus*, p. 181). See also Camus' comments on optimism and pessimism in a 1951 interview, in *Lyrical and Critical Essays*, pp.351–2.
147 Camus, *Lyrical and Critical Essays*, p.335.
148 Ibid., p.336.
149 Meursault, to be sure, does lie at various points, sometimes with serious repercussions, as when he agrees to write a sham letter for his neighbor Raymond, enabling the latter to win back and humiliate his estranged Arab mistress (see *The Stranger*, p.40). Camus' point, however, is that Meursault "says what he is, he refuses to hide his feelings" (*Lyrical and Critical Essays*, p.336). Meursault's integrity, then, lies in a refusal to profess feelings (e.g., of grief, of love, of remorse) that he does not have, remaining faithful to his way of experiencing the world and speaking 'his truth' in a direct, if not naïve, way, which is partly why many around him feel ill at ease.
150 Cf. the prosecutor's description of Meursault as "an inhuman monster wholly without moral sense" (Camus, *The Stranger*, p.120), a description echoed by Jean Onimus, *Albert Camus and Christianity*, trans. Emmett Parker (Dublin: Gill and Macmillan, 1970), p.67.
151 Camus, *Lyrical and Critical Essays*, pp.336–7. A similar pattern of thought is present in *The Myth of Sisyphus*, where Camus asks whether suicide is the only or best response to the meaninglessness of existence. His answer, in short, is that even within the depths of nihilism and absurdity can be found "a lucid invitation to live and to create" (Preface). In the course of charting a way out of nihilism, he offers (in Part I of the essay, "An Absurd Reasoning") a number of 'definitions' or clarifications of the experience of absurdity, one of which refers to "the cruel mathematics" of death, the recognition of its definitive and final character (p.21). But the experience of absurdity, Camus goes on to say, is one that we should not seek to erase or evade (through, e.g., suicide, whether physical or intellectual), but must confront and struggle with it—and this entails the rejection of false hopes, including the religion-inspired effort to imagine and live for a life beyond this life. Having rejected any accommodation with the absurd, and living 'without appeal' and with the awareness that all our noontime passions are 'for nothing,' Camus contends that we need not be reduced to despair. At this point he turns to mythology rather than philosophy, and in particular to his model of the absurd hero: Sisyphus. In response to his wretched condition, Sisyphus is not crushed but consciously faces his fate, rising above it through scorn and revolt. Camus

ends with the image of Sisyphus at the foot of the mountain, ready once more to roll the rock upwards: "The struggle itself toward the heights is enough to fill a man's heart. One must imagine Sisyphus happy" (p.111).

Bibliography

Anderson, O. "The Feminism of T. H. Green: A Late-Victorian Success Story?" *History of Political Thought, 12* (1991), 671–93.

Anderson, T. "Sartre's Early Ethics and the Ontology of *Being and Nothingness*," in C. Guignon (ed.), *The Existentialists: Critical Essays on Kierkegaard, Nietzsche, Heidegger, and Sartre* (Lanham, MD: Rowman and Littlefield Publishers, 2004), pp.135–52.

Blattner, W. "Heidegger: The Existential Analytic of Dasein," in S. Crowell (ed.), *The Cambridge Companion to Existentialism* (Cambridge: Cambridge University Press, 2012), pp.158–77. https://doi.org/10.1017/ccol9780521513340.009

Boethius. *The Consolation of Philosophy*, trans. V. E. Watts (London: Penguin, 1969).

Bosanquet, B. "On the True Conception of Another World," in *Essays and Addresses*, 2nd edn (London: Swan Sonnenschein, 1891), pp.92–107.

Bosanquet, B. "The Reality of the General Will," in Bosanquet (ed.), *Aspects of the Social Problem* (London: Macmillan and Co., 1895), pp.319–32.

Bosanquet, B. *Principle of Individuality and Value* (London: Macmillan, 1912).

Bosanquet, B. "Reply," in H. Wildon Carr (ed.), *Life and Infinite Individuality* (London: Williams and Norgate, 1918), pp.179–94.

Bosanquet, B. "Unvisited Tombs," in *Some Suggestions in Ethics* (London: Macmillan, 1919), pp.66–87.

Bosanquet, B. "On 'Doubting the Reality of Evil,'" in *Some Suggestions in Ethics*, pp.88–125.

Bosanquet, B. *The Value and Destiny of the Individual* (London: Macmillan, 1923).

Bosanquet, B., A. S. Pringle-Pattison, G. F. Stout and R. B. Haldane. "Symposium: Do Finite Individuals Possess a Substantive or an Adjectival Mode of Being?" *Proceedings of the Aristotelian Society, 18* (1917–18), 479–581.

Bradley, F. H. *Ethical Studies*, 2nd edn (London: Oxford University Press, 1962, originally published 1876).

Bradley, F. H. *Appearance and Reality*, 1st edn (Oxford: Oxford University Press, 1893); 2nd edn, 9th impression (Oxford: Clarendon Press, 1930).

Burrell, D. *Faith and Freedom: An Interfaith Perspective* (Oxford: Blackwell, 2004). https://doi.org/10.1002/9780470753125

Caird, J. "Corporate Immortality," in *University Sermons Preached before the University of Glasgow 1873–1898* (Glasgow: James MacLehose and Sons, 1898), pp.176–95.

Camus, A. *Lyrical and Critical Essays*, trans. E. Conroy Kennedy, ed. P. Thody (New York: Vintage Books, 1970).

Camus, A. *The Stranger*, trans. S. Gilbert (New York: Alfred A. Knopf, 1974).
Camus, A. *The Myth of Sisyphus*, trans. J. O'Brien (London: Penguin, 2000).
Camus, A. *Notebooks: 1951–1959*, trans. R. Bloom (Chicago, IL: Ivan R. Dee, 2008).
Coburn, R. C. "Professor Malcolm on God," *Australasian Journal of Philosophy, 41* (1963), 143–62.
Davies, B. "Simplicity," in C. Taliaferro and C. Meister (eds), *The Cambridge Companion to Christian Philosophical Theology* (Cambridge: Cambridge University Press, 2010), pp.31–45. https://doi.org/10.1017/ccol9780521514330.003
Eliot, T. S. *Selected Prose of T. S. Eliot*, ed. F. Kermode (New York: Harcourt Brace Jovanovich, 1975).
Flynn, T. R. "Sartre," in S. Critchley and W. R. Schroeder (eds), *A Companion to Continental Philosophy* (Malden, MA: Blackwell, 1999), pp.256–68.
Gowans, C. *Philosophy of the Buddha* (London: Routledge, 2003). https://doi.org/10.4324/9780203480793
Hartshorne, C. *The Divine Relativity: A Social Conception of God* (New Haven, CT: Yale University Press, 1948).
Hartshorne, C. *The Zero Fallacy and Other Essays in Neoclassical Philosophy*, ed. M. Valady (Chicago, IL: Open Court, 1997).
Heidegger, M. *Being and Time*, trans. J. Macquarrie and E. Robinson (Malden, MA: Blackwell Publishing, 1962).
Heidegger, M. *History of the Concept of Time: Prolegomena*, trans. T. Kisiel (Bloomington: Indiana University Press, 1992).
Hume, D. *A Treatise of Human Nature*, ed. E. C. Mossner (London: Penguin, 1984).
Kierkegaard, S. *Fear and Trembling; Repetition*, ed. and trans. H. V. Hong and E. H. Hong (Princeton, NJ: Princeton University Press, 1983). https://doi.org/10.1515/9781400846955
Kierkegaard, S. *Concluding Unscientific Postscript to 'Philosophical Fragments,'* ed. and trans. H. V. Hong and E. H. Hong (Princeton, NJ: Princeton University Press, 1992). https://doi.org/10.1515/9781400847037
Kierkegaard, S. *Papers and Journals: A Selection*, trans. A. Hannay (London: Penguin, 1996).
Macquarrie, J. *Existentialism* (Harmondsworth: Penguin, 1973).
Mander, W. J. "In Defence of the Eternal Consciousness," in M. Dimova-Cookson and W. J. Mander (eds), *T. H. Green: Ethics, Metaphysics, and Political Philosophy* (Oxford: Clarendon Press, 2006), pp.187–206. https://doi.org/10.1093/acprof:oso/9780199271665.003.0008
Mander, W. J., *British Idealism: A History* (Oxford: Oxford University Press, 2011). https://doi.org/10.1093/acprof:oso/9780199559299.001.0001
Mulhall, S. *Routledge Philosophy Guidebook to Heidegger and 'Being and Time,'* 2nd edn (London: Routledge, 2005). https://doi.org/10.4324/9780203003084
Nietzsche, F. *Twilight of the Idols and The Anti-Christ*, trans. R. J. Hollingdale (London: Penguin, 1990).

Nietzsche, F. *Ecce Homo*, trans. R. J. Hollingdale (London: Penguin, 1992).

Nietzsche, F. *Daybreak: Thoughts on the Prejudices of Morality*, trans. R. J. Hollingdale, ed. M. Clark and B. Leiter (Cambridge: Cambridge University Press, 1997).

Onimus, J. *Albert Camus and Christianity*, trans. E. Parker (Dublin: Gill and Macmillan, 1970).

Pringle-Pattison, A. S. (as Seth, A.) *Hegelianism and Personality*, 2nd edn (Edinburgh: William Blackwood and Sons, 1893). (Works by Pringle-Pattison published prior to 1898 were published under the name of Andrew Seth.)

Pringle-Pattison, A. S. *Man's Place in the Cosmos and Other Essays*, 2nd edn (Edinburgh: William Blackwood and Sons, 1902).

Pringle-Pattison, A. S. *The Idea of God in the Light of Recent Philosophy*, 2nd edn (New York: Oxford University Press, 1920).

Pringle-Pattison, A. S. *The Idea of Immortality* (Oxford: Clarendon Press, 1922).

Sartre, J.-P. *Existentialism and Humanism*, trans. P. Mairet (London: Methuen and Co., 1948).

Sartre, J.-P. *The Transcendence of the Ego: An Existentialist Theory of Consciousness*, trans. F. Williams and R. Kirkpatrick (New York: Hill and Wang, 1960).

Sartre, J.-P. *Between Existentialism and Marxism*, trans. J. Matthews (London: NLB, 1974).

Sartre, J.-P. *'No Exit' and Three Other Plays* (New York: Vintage, 1989).

Sartre, J.-P. *Notebooks for an Ethics*, trans. D. Pellauer (Chicago, IL: The University of Chicago Press, 1992).

Simhony, A. "'To Set Free the Idea of the Self': Bosanquet's Relational Individual," in W. J. Mander and S. Panagakou (eds), *British Idealism and the Concept of the Self* (London: Palgrave Macmillan, 2016), pp.201–24. https://doi.org/10.1057/978-1-137-46671-6_10

Webb, C. C. B. "Bernard Bosanquet's Philosophy of Religion," *The Hibbert Journal, 22* (1923), 75–96.

Whitehead, A. N. *Process and Reality: An Essay in Cosmology*, corrected edn, ed. D. R. Griffin and D. W. Sherburne (New York: The Free Press, 1985).

Williams, B. "The Makropulos Case: Reflections on the Tedium of Immortality," in *Problems of the Self* (Cambridge: Cambridge University Press, 1973), pp.82–100. https://doi.org/10.1017/cbo9780511621253.008

4 Concluding Remarks

4.1

Where does the preceding interplay between existentialism and idealism leave us? The idealist conception of value and reality is, of course, predicated on an unabashedly metaphysical outlook where the most basic principle or element that holds the key to all of life's mysteries (what the Presocratics called the *archê*) is 'mind.' Everything, including the physical world, exists only as an appearance to or expression of mind, whether the mind-like nature of ultimate reality is conceived in nonpersonal terms as the Absolute, or in personal, theistic terms as God. Either way, this 'ideal' reality is the fundamental basis of all there is and the goal towards which all human life strives. The existentialist, as we saw, sees matters quite differently, regarding the values that inform the well-lived life—values such as authenticity, integrity, individuality and autonomy—as presupposing a metaphysical picture of the world that is 'Godforsaken.' This is a term S. J. McGrath has used to describe Heidegger's phenomenological project,[1] where any appeal to the divine is refused when developing a 'hermeneutics of facticity,' a way of understanding the concrete configurations of what it is to be-in-the-world, a way of setting out and interpreting the determinate and definite features of Dasein. This, in turn, brings us to Heidegger's insistence on religious neutrality and his rejection of 'Christian philosophy' as "a round square and a misunderstanding,"[2] so that any attempt to explore the meaning of being by reference to a divine or infinite being is ruled out in advance. The question of being can only be (genuinely) pursued by way of (phenomenological) ontology, not one of the ontic sciences such as theology. And from this ontological perspective, there is no access to anything beyond time or any postmortem life, in which case being is understood as thoroughly temporal and finite. The very idea of an afterlife is therefore

DOI: 10.4324/9781003378624-4

dismissed from the outset, or at least bracketed from philosophical consideration.[3]

Rather than defending Heidegger's methodology, my aim here is only to highlight the disparate starting-points of existentialists and idealists. For the former, we find ourselves 'thrown' into a thoroughly contingent, if not alien and absurd, world, lacking any God-given meaning, in which case the authentic confrontation with death requires the recognition of our inescapable finitude and mortality.[4] But for the idealist, the world is overflowing with meaning, where this encompasses the possibility of transcending death through a process of 'self-realization' (adhering in this respect to Hick's dictum of 'no theodicy without eschatology'). The Welsh idealist, Henry Jones, expressed this well in a memorable passage from his 1905 lecture, *The Immortality of the Soul in the Poems of Tennyson and Browning*:

> Ever since the days of Lessing and Kant mankind has been travelling away from the narrow infinitude and hard-lined limitedness of the days of Hume. Philosophers and poets alike—almost all of the greatest of them—Fichte and Schelling, Hegel and Goethe, Carlyle and Wordsworth, Shelley, Tennyson, and Browning, have steeped the present life in the life to come. Thought and sense, spirit and nature interpenetrate; time is saturated with eternity. The universe is spirit-woven, God is immanent in it, and every meanest object is in its way "filled full of magical music, as they freight a star with light."[5]

4.2

But how are we to choose between these competing visions: the gloomy world of "hard-lined limitedness" of naturalists like Hume and existentialists like Heidegger and Sartre, versus the world of the philosophical idealists and romantic poets, which hides beneath its surface "magical music" and "intimations of immortality" (to borrow from Wordsworth)?

Rather than plumping for one side over the other, I want to take a leaf out of John Caputo's little book, *On Religion*, where in the course of defending a postmodern take on religious faith he discusses two similar rival worldviews. The first of these he calls 'the tragic sense of life,' a view of the world that is "distressing," "stark and unlovely, indeed utterly loveless."[6] The answer, on this view, to the question 'Does anyone know or care that we are here?' is a resounding 'No!'[7] There is no higher being taking providential control of the world and bestowing it with purpose. Rather, as Nietzsche thought, we are "just so many little animals scurrying across the surface of a little planet in a far-off distant corner of the universe inventing proud words for ourselves—like 'the love of God.'"[8] Eventually, "the little planet will run out of steam and sink back into its sun and be reduced to ash, and the little animals and their noble words will die."[9] Although Caputo only references Nietzsche in this context, one is also reminded of Bertrand Russell's equally poignant expression of this outlook in 'A Free Man's Worship.' The world disclosed by science, Russell contends, is one where

...no fire, no heroism, no intensity of thought and feeling, can preserve an individual life beyond the grave;...all the labours of the ages, all the devotion, all the inspiration, all the noonday brightness of human genius, are destined to extinction in the vast death of the solar system, and...the whole temple of Man's achievement must inevitably be buried beneath the debris of a universe in ruins.[10]

The truth of this outlook is for Nietzsche and Russell practically beyond dispute, yet Caputo argues that it is not the only game in town. There is also a 'religious sense of life' which "is forged over and against this tragic sense."[11] The religious vision is expressed, by Caputo at least, as the

faith that there is something that lifts us above the blind force of things, a mind in all this mindlessness, a heart in all this heartlessness. That there is *something*...or *someone*...who stands by us when we are up against the worst, who stands by others, by the least among us.[12]

Caputo's postmodern twist to this comparison of the tragic and the religious is that there is "a radical and inescapable fluctuation or 'undecidability'" between the two perspectives.[13] As he goes on to explain: "There is no cognitively definitive way to settle what is what or what is going on, no way to adjudicate their dispute, no knockdown argument for the one and against the other."[14] Without wishing to enter into the details, Caputo is here drawing upon his 'radical hermeneutics,' a hermeneutics radicalized by deconstruction so as to produce a structural 'blindness' or non-knowing expressed by Caputo in terms of the thesis that

we are not (as far as we know) born into this world hard-wired to Being Itself, or Truth Itself, or the Good Itself, that we are not vessels of a Divine or World-Historical super-force that has chosen us as its earthly instruments, and that, when we open our mouths, it is we who speak, not something Bigger and Better than we. We have not been given privileged access to The Secret, to some big capitalized know-it-all Secret, not as far as we know. (If we have, it has been kept secret from me.) The secret is, there is no Secret...[15]

In light of our awareness of this secret, Caputo says, "we must all 'fess up' that we do not know who we are or what is going on, not 'Really,' not in some 'Deep Way,' although we all have our views."[16] For Caputo, then, neither the tragic vision nor the religious one can be accepted as the final truth; instead, each should be seen as merely one perspective or interpretation among others, and—most important of all—there is an inescapable *undecidability* between them. Borrowing from Derrida, 'undecidability' does not refer to some kind of psychological indecision or paralysis ('If only I had more information or evidence, I could make up my mind!'), but rather points to a more fundamental feature of judgement and decision-making, whereby some measure of risk and faith is unavoidable. This is particularly evident in life-commitments (such as marriage, or conversion to a religion) that go beyond 'programmability,' requiring something other than making a decision mechanically by (e.g.) following an algorithm or decision-procedure.

Given such undecidability, the religious vision is permanently "haunted and disturbed from within" by the nihilism of the tragic vision. Like a spectre that can never be killed off, the tragic view forever haunts the religious follower, reminding them that what they believe is based on faith, not knowledge, keeping them honest and on their toes, challenging their tendency to "triumphalism and self-enclosure," if not also intolerance and violence.[17]

4.3

I have no intention of unreservedly endorsing Caputo's postmodern philosophy of religion,[18] but there is nonetheless something salutary about his 'confession of faith'—or what I'd prefer to call the Socratic knowledge of our lack of knowledge. Idealism, however, has not been hospitable to such thoroughgoing scepticism. A case in point are the British Idealists, whose philosophy was often seen as an antidote to the rise of religious scepticism during the Victorian 'crisis of faith.' In an age that was "destitute of faith, and terrified at scepticism," as Thomas Carlyle put it,[19] the British Idealists sought to salvage what they took to be the essence or spirit of the crumbling creeds, where this meant not only demythologizing doctrinal, supernaturalistic religion but also standing opposed to both positivistic atheism and the agnosticism of Spenser, Huxley, Clifford and their like.[20] While these agnostics insisted on the incapacity of human reason to uncover the nature of ultimate reality, their idealist counterparts had faith in the potential of philosophical inquiry to rigorously penetrate appearances and provide a secure basis for our values and hopes. As John Caird, under the influence of Hegel, stated: "If you begin with reason and criticism, you must go on with them... The wounds of reason can only be healed by reason."[21]

The sceptic, typically, refuses any such faith in reason, detecting in it a hubris or lack of humility, a vain attempt to overreach the limits of the human condition. Recall Camus' injunction to reject magical cures and instead "live with one's ailment." The failure to do so could be regarded, as it was by the ancient Greeks, as an attempted breach of the ideal of 'measure,' the universal limits inherent in nature. Transgressions of these limits, whether by gods or mortals, threaten to overturn the order of the world and are therefore swiftly punished by the dreaded Erinyes. It is even possible to see this in religious terms, as does Kierkegaard in his satire of Hegel's claims to finality and completeness. But Kierkegaard too, as Camus points out, wants to be cured and takes the leap, and in doing so the 'equilibrium' between the world's irrationality and human longing is lost. As television playwright Dennis Potter has said, "Now that to me isn't religion... religion to me has always been the wound, not the bandage."[22]

Existentialism arguably does a much better job at keeping the wound open than does idealism. This is due in part to the recognition in existentialism of the irreducible ambiguity, richness and diversity of experience, which is why many existentialists turned away from the kind of rational reinterpretation or systematization of phenomena undertaken by philosophers and looked instead to literature and the arts as more faithful expressions of existential realities such as the singularity of others: Sartre, for example, writes plays, Camus publishes novels, Beauvoir also writes novels as well as a string of autobiographical volumes, while the famous 'turn' (*die Kehre*) in Heidegger involves a move away from Western metaphysics to a belief in the power of poetry, especially that of Hölderlin and Rilke, to unveil the mysteries of Being.

Beauvoir went so far as to think of herself as a literary author rather than a philosopher. Even so, her literary work is infused with philosophical reflections: her novel *She Came to Stay* (1943), for example, takes as its epigraph Hegel's statement that, "Each consciousness pursues the death of the other," and goes on to explore the conflictual nature of intersubjectivity. The freedom and identity of the three leading characters—Françoise, Pierre and Xavière (roughly mirroring the real-life love triangle of Beauvoir, Sartre and the young and fiery Olga Kosakiewicz)—becomes increasingly entangled and compromised over the course of the novel, until in the end Françoise feels she has no other means of reclaiming her happiness except through eliminating (murdering, in fact) the interloper, Xavière. Relationality is inescapable, as the idealists taught, but it is also inescapably oppressive and violent.[23] The philosophical dimension is also prominent in Beauvoir's autobiographies, which fulfil the aim of her lifelong existentialist project, described by Toril Moi as: "to break down the distinction between philosophy and life so as to endow life with the truth and necessity of philosophy and philosophy with the excitement and passion of life."[24] This dissolution of univocal being and retrieval of plurivocal 'betweenness' becomes a leading strand in Beauvoir's 1947 work, *The Ethics of Ambiguity*, where she points out that "from the very beginning, existentialism defined itself as a philosophy of ambiguity."[25] Most philosophers and most ethical systems, she claims, have sought to evade or eliminate the tragic ambiguity of the human condition, an ambiguity arising from the tension between facticity and transcendence, between the givens of our situation and the opportunities and choices to reach beyond these givens. The goal, however, is to maintain the tension created by the interplay of these poles and others like it (such as matter and mind, self and other), rather than fleeing from the resultant antinomies and anxieties by making recourse to absolutes like God and Humanity. For it is only by recognizing the ambiguity of existence, only by acknowledging "that its meaning is never fixed, that it must be constantly won,"[26] that a genuine ethics is possible. This is an ethics founded upon the value of (what Beauvoir calls) 'moral freedom,' a freedom forged in the anguished realization that, in the absence of absolutes, the burden of responsibility falls entirely on us: *contra* Dostoevsky, if there is no God, the gravity of our choices is only magnified.[27] If ethics is not anchored in God but in finite subjects lacking fixed foundations, the ethics that follows can only be one of ambiguity, one that "resides in the painfulness of an indefinite questioning,"[28] as we try to navigate contingencies without seeking cover in certitudes.

The sceptical stance thus runs deep in existentialism.[29] But it does so not merely as an intellectual pose of suspending judgement on the truth of a proposition, or conceding that not everything is knowable or expressible in discursive thought—something that, to be fair, many idealists also rejected: for Bradley, for example, reality outstrips thought, so that abstraction is necessarily falsification. What British idealists often overlooked, however, are the existential possibilities of scepticism, seeing it as a way of life that provides an alternative to traditional religious affiliation as well as ordinary ways of practising philosophy. The ancient sceptics knew this well. Pyrrho of Elis (*c*.360–*c*.270 BCE), around twenty years Aristotle's junior, notoriously advocated a 'life without belief': against his critics, he argued that such a life is not only possible, but is the only sure path to happiness. He thought that once we admit *isostheneia*—the view that the reasons in favour of any given belief are always equally good (or equally bad) as the reasons against that belief—and therefore stop trying to resolve the endless philosophical disputes, we can finally attain *ataraxia*: peace of mind, freedom from disturbance.

But we need not go all the way with Pyrrho, who reputedly withdrew trust in the veracity of ordinary impressions to the extent that he would take no precautions against oncoming carts, precipices or dogs, and was kept out of harm's way only by the help of friends.[30] The point, rather, is to recognize the existential, as well as theoretical, benefits of scepticism, and so to treat it as a holistic undertaking. Lesley Hazleton, in *Agnostic: A Spirited Manifesto*, expresses the character of this kind of scepticism well:

> The agnostic stance defies artificial straight lines such as that drawn between belief and unbelief, and shakes off the insistence that it come down on one side or the other. It is free-spirited, thoughtful, and independent-minded—not at all in the wishy-washy I-don't-knowness that atheists often accuse it of being... I stand tall in my agnosticism, because the essence of it is not merely not-knowing, but something far more challenging and infinitely more intriguing: the magnificent oxymoron inherent in the concept of unknowability. This is the acknowledgement that not everything may be knowable, and that not all questions have definitive answers—certainly not ones as crudely put as the existence or non-existence of God.[31]

But this remains too negative a characterization, and doesn't get to the heart of the agnostic stance, as Hazleton explains:

> At its best, however, agnosticism goes further: it takes a spirited delight in not knowing. And this delight is no boorish disdain for knowledge and intellect. Rather, it's a recognition that we need

room for mystery, for the imagination, for things sensed but not proven, intuited but not defined—room in which to explore and entertain possibilities instead of heading straight for a safe seat at one end or the other of a falsely created spectrum.[32]

Hazleton points to the increasing tendency of younger Americans to self-identify as 'spiritual but not religious' as a promising move away from traditional forms of commitment and conviction, and towards a more open-ended and sceptical orientation.[33] "In fact," Hazleton writes,

> I am tired of conviction... Conviction is not only to be convinced; it's also to be convicted, like a prisoner in his cell. It is to close one's mind, to nail oneself down beyond a shadow of doubt—a turn of phrase that sees doubt as a threat...[34]

Hazleton, therefore, presents her book as an 'agnostic manifesto,' one that offers no answers and certainties but only questions and quests. Even agnosticism is not something she wishes to preach or convert her readers to. "The last thing needed," she says, "is yet another pompously 'complete' system of thought and belief demanding adherents to some sort of party line."[35] If there is anything she does preach, it is the values of agnosticism: humility, vulnerability, insecurity, openness, spontaneity and adventure, values lost or diminished in grand philosophical structures.[36]

4.4

I will conclude with two literary exemplifications of the kind of scepticism that philosophy—particularly the philosophy of idealism and contemporary philosophy of religion—stands sorely in need of. Readers are unlikely to have encountered either of these previously, which is partly why I thought to include them here. The first concerns the modern Greek poet and novelist, Aris Alexandrou (1922–78). An unconventional leftist, Alexandrou spent much of his life in jail or in exile for his refusal to submit to political authority. Soon after his acclaimed and only novel, *Το κιβώτιο* ('The Mission Box'), was published in 1974, he was asked in an interview: "Which political party do you belong to?" The year of publication is significant, as this was the beginning of Greece's transformation from a military dictatorship (in power since 1967) to the restoration of (participatory, pluralistic) democracy. But in a country ravaged by dissension and war, markers of (especially political and religious) affiliation still loomed large, as did feelings of bitterness and resentment in groups (like the communists) who had until recently been excluded and marginalized. And so it is all the more impressive that Alexandrou, when asked to display his political colours, responded: "I don't belong to any party, nor to any political group. I am not a member of any church. I am not a follower of any religion. As I've said before, Δεσμώτης τῆδε ἴσταμαι τοῖς ἔνδον ῥήμασι πειθόμενος'."[37] This ancient Greek expression—which can be translated as "Here I stand committed, abiding by the voice within"—has something of the spirit of Socrates about it. Like Socrates, Alexandrou enjoins us to listen to our inner *daimon*, forging our own path and thinking for ourselves rather than letting others think for us; and to follow the 'gadfly of Athens' in testing pretensions to knowledge and wisdom in others, while being ourselves prepared to "go wherever the wind of the argument carries us."

The second literary figure is Alexandrou's contemporary, Tasos Leivaditis (1922–88), one of the unacknowledged greats of Modern Greek literature. Leivaditis' early poetry was heavily influenced by a doctrinaire communist outlook and his participation in the resistance movement during World War II and the ensuing civil war in Greece (1946–49), which led to his detention and exile in various camps across the Aegean islands. In the aftermath of the defeat of the left in the civil war, Leivaditis gradually turned away from his previous political commitments toward a bleaker, disillusioned poetic vision permeated with existentialist concerns and quasi-religious imagery. Even as the religious tones and themes become more prominent, there is never a desire for creedal or confessional allegiance, but a striving to break free from orthodoxies of all kinds, political and theological. Leivaditis' postwar world is one of alienation and oblivion, "a world torn asunder / with a derelict God going around from door to door / begging for his existence."[38] The journey for meaning is not a communal or comradely one, as it was before, but a lonely and despairing search haunted by lost causes and ideals, "broken dreams and dead music"[39] that keep the poet up all night. There is a passionate, even erotic "hankering after God"[40] in Leivaditis' later work, often recalling the apophatic stream in Eastern Orthodox theology and spirituality, with its emphasis on the mystery and incomprehensibility of God. But the apophaticism of the Orthodox Church is circumscribed by its 'cataphaticism,' its authoritative positive pronouncements—stumbling-blocks to a generation, like Leivaditis,' betrayed and often persecuted and murdered by ideologies of both left and right. If any divinity remains from these ruins, it is the one disclosed in the 'books' of the French-Jewish writer, Edmond Jabès, for whom "God is a questioning of God."[41] This sacred but sceptical, endless and direction-less wandering is expressed in characteristic fashion in one of Leivaditis' poems from his 1985 masterpiece, *Violets for a Season*, and I will end by quoting it here in full:

Lonesome Steps

> There exists, they say, a great adventure for each of us, but where will we find it?
> for now we leaf through the old calendars in case we save something from the years —
> truly, what goes on in reality? who remembers what happened yesterday? everything hazy, confused
> in the morning I walk over the rubble of two wars in order to get to the kitchen for coffee
> vagrants watch the trains departing and their eyes are orphaned for a moment
> and it is not rain on the glass-enclosed waiting rooms at the stations but the unfulfilled journeys that are weeping
> drunkards stagger under the weight of the infinite
> outside the orphanages persecuted fairytales fall silent
> and the woman by the window is so sad that she is ready to depart for the sky
> everything hazy, confused — others construct from us a face for their own use
> who are we? nobody knows and only sometimes in our nightmares do we find part of our true self —
> hands that crumbled in awkward gestures
> violet-coloured compassion of the twilight which spreads a bit of regal lace on homes for the aged
> the divine right of the poor over the possessions of others
> the lonesome steps of a passerby which remind you of your entire life
> and my father, dead for so many years, comes each night and gives me advice in my sleep, "but father," I tell him, "you forget that we are the same age"
> oh my lost generation — we took great roads, we remained in the middle
> the hour of our death is written on all clocks
> childhood friends, where are you? with whom will I now continue my wanderings in the infinite? the grown-ups are in the cafés

the crickets in the evening are attempting to pronounce the
    ineffable
mother would open letters with her hairpin
our life is a mystery which we cannot share
a sorrow in the afternoon like the aroma of old books
and each time we pass by a pedestrian it is as though we are
    saying "goodbye" to the whole of life —
do you remember our erotic moments, Anna? your sex like a half-
    opened shell laid there by a distant tempest
your breasts two small heliotropes in unforgettable mornings —
revolutionaries are concerned about the future, lovers about the
    past, poets have taken responsibility for both
someday I will commit suicide in dramatic fashion: with hushed
    words from old conspiratorial days,
ah, life, a handshake with the infinite before you are lost forever
children know well that the impossible is the best solution
while two musicians play the accordion in the depths of dusk for
    luck
        and their hats swim,
        shipwrecked in music.[42]

Notes

1 S. J. McGrath, *The Early Heidegger and Medieval Philosophy: Phenomenology for the Godforsaken* (Washington, DC: The Catholic University of America Press, 2006).

2 Heidegger, *Introduction to Metaphysics*, trans. Gregory Field and Richard Polt (New Haven, CT: Yale University Press, 2000), p.8.

3 It is an open question, however, to what degree Heidegger himself abided by his methodological neutrality on religious matters, or whether many of his important ideas are drawn from, and depend upon, some religious context. On Heidegger's stated neutrality on the question of life after death, see *Being and Time* §49, p.292. But as Paul Gorner notes, "how plausible is this neutrality? If death is the possibility of the impossibility of *any* comportment to anything then the idea of an afterlife surely makes no sense" (*Heidegger's 'Being and Time': An Introduction*, Cambridge: Cambridge University Press, 2007, p.125, n20, emphasis in original). For further discussion of Heidegger's methodology, see my "Philosophy and Religious Commitment."

4 Here, I should note, I am restricting existentialism to its secular or atheistic variety, which followed Nietzsche in philosophizing in light of the death of God, and was chiefly represented by Heidegger and the French contingent of Sartre, Beauvoir and Camus. Parallel with this group there was a theistic, or at least religious, stream of existentialism that followed Kierkegaard in developing an existential approach to religious faith. Members of this latter group included Karl Jaspers, Martin Buber, Nicolas Berdyaev, Reinhold Niebuhr, and Gabriel Marcel.

5 Henry Jones, *The Immortality of the Soul in the Poems of Tennyson and Browning* (London: Philip Green, 1905), p.20. The verse "filled full of magical music, as they freight a star with light" is from Robert Browning's 1835 poem, "Paracelsus" (Part V, 114–16).

6 John D. Caputo, *On Religion*, 2nd edn (Abingdon: Routledge, 2019), p.182.

7 Ibid.

8 Ibid., p.183.

9 Ibid.

10 Bertrand Russell, "A Free Man's Worship" (originally published 1903), in *Mysticism and Logic and Other Essays* (London: Unwin Books, 1970), p.41. Bosanquet, interestingly, responded to Russell's essay, calling it an instance of "the unhappy consciousness in the plainest form," as it seeks to construct a positive and rational structure upon a foundation of despair. See Bosanquet, *Value and Destiny of the Individual*, p.319.

11 Caputo, *On Religion*, p.184.

12 Ibid., p.190, emphases in original.

13 Ibid., p.188.

14 Ibid., pp.188–9.

15 Caputo, *More Radical Hermeneutics: On Not Knowing Who We Are* (Bloomington: Indiana University Press, 2000), p.1. Cf. Caputo's discussion of 'the Secret' on pp.19–26 in *On Religion*, where he states: "The secret is that there is no Secret, no capitalized Know-it-all Breakthrough Principle or Revelation that lays things out the way they Really Are and thereby lays to rest the conflict of interpretations" (p.23).

16 Caputo, *On Religion*, p.189.

17 Ibid., p.185.

18 For a critique of Caputo's postmodern philosophy of religion, see my "Postmodern Approaches to Religion," in Graham Oppy (ed.), *The Routledge Handbook of Contemporary Philosophy of Religion* (London: Routledge, 2015), pp.32–50.

19 Carlyle, review of J.G. Lockhart, *Memoirs of the Life of Sir Walter Scott*, in *The London and Westminster Review* (January 1838), p.168.

20 See, for example, Bosanquet's paper, "Are We Agnostics?" in his *The Civilization of Christendom and Other Studies* (London: Swann Sonnenschein, 1893), pp.127–59. This was written in the wake of Huxley's recent invention of the term 'agnosticism.' Bosanquet complains of the 'thinness of doctrine' that emerges out of the agnostic stance, which "cannot give place to a richer culture until the attitude of ignorance is exchanged for an attitude of knowledge" (pp.136–7).

21 John Caird, "David Hume," in *University Addresses* (Glasgow: James MacLehose and Sons, 1898), p.189.

22 Dennis Potter, "An Interview with Melvyn Bragg (April 1994)," in *Seeing the Blossom: Two Interviews, a Lecture and a Story* (London: Faber and Faber, 1994), p.5. This interview was conducted soon after Potter was diagnosed with cancer, from which he died in June of that year. As the context makes clear, the specific kind of religion he is here repudiating is one that includes such things as postmortem rewards and punishments and theodical justifications of suffering.

Concluding Remarks 91

23 See Simone de Beauvoir, *She Came to Stay*, trans. Yvonne Moyse and Roger Senhouse (London: Harper Perennial, 2006); originally published in 1943 as *L'Invitée*.

24 Toril Moi, *Simone de Beauvoir: The Making of an Intellectual Woman* (Oxford: Blackwell, 1994), p.147. On the ways in which *She Came to Stay* exemplifies the 'life is philosophy' stance, see Ashley King Scheu, "The Viability of the Philosophical Novel: The Case of Simone de Beauvoir's *She Came to Stay*," *Hypatia, 27* (2012), 791–809.

25 Beauvoir, *The Ethics of Ambiguity*, trans. Bernard Frechtman (New York: The Citadel Press, 1970), p.9. This was originally published in 1947 as *Pour une morale de l'ambiguïté*.

26 Ibid., p.129.

27 Ibid., pp.15–16.

28 Ibid., p.133.

29 Heidegger, for instance, defines Dasein as a being which questions, and which questions above all its own being. As Robert Wicks explains, "Human beings are thrown into the world, in other words, with a dominating question mark inscribed into their being" (*Modern French Philosophy: From Existentialism to Postmodernism*, Oxford: Oneworld, 2003, p.40). Wicks goes on to show how Sartre, inspired by the Heideggerian view as well as the Cartesian method of universal doubt, brings these two approaches together in conceiving human beings as self-doubting, self-questioning beings.

30 See Diogenes Laertius, *Lives of Eminent Philosophers*, book 9, §62.

31 Hazleton, *Agnostic: A Spirited Manifesto* (New York: Riverhead Books, 2016), pp.4–6.

32 Ibid., p.6.

33 Ibid., pp.14–15.

34 Ibid., p.15. See also pp.59–60, where conviction is analysed as a product of insecurity and frailty. A similar critique of conviction is made by Nietzsche in *The Antichrist*, §§54–55.

35 Hazleton, *Agnostic*, p.21.

36 Ibid., pp.49–50. For further development, see N. N. Trakakis, "How To Be An Agnostic," *European Journal for Philosophy of Religion, 13* (2021), 179–94.

37 Aris Alexandrou, Ἔξω ἀπ᾽ τά δόντια (1937–1975), 2nd edn (Athens: Ypsilon, 1982), p.181, translation mine.

38 Leivaditis, "Genesis (Version 3)," *Poems: 1958–1964*, in *Poetry, vol. 1: 1950–1966* [in Greek] (Athens: Metronomos, 2015), p.392, translation mine.

39 Leivaditis, "Years of Fire," in *The Blind Man with the Lamp*, trans. N. N. Trakakis (Limni, Evia: Denise Harvey, 2014), p.87.

40 Leivaditis, "Scenes from the Station," in *The Blind Man with the Lamp*, p.8.

41 Edmond Jabès, *The Book of Questions, volume 1*, trans. Rosmarie Waldrop (Hanover, NH: Wesleyan University Press, 1991), p.138.

42 Leivaditis, *Violets for a Season*, trans. N. N. Trakakis (Northfield, MN: Red Dragonfly Press, 2017), pp.54–5 (modified). This work was originally published in Greek in 1985.

Bibliography

Alexandrou, A. Ἔξω ἀπ' τά δόντια *(1937–1975)*, 2nd edn (Athens: Ypsilon, 1982).

Bosanquet, B. "Are We Agnostics?" in *The Civilization of Christendom and Other Studies* (London: Swann Sonnenschein, 1893), pp.127–59.

Bosanquet, B. *The Value and Destiny of the Individual* (London: Macmillan, 1923).

Caird, J. "David Hume," in *University Addresses* (Glasgow: James MacLehose and Sons, 1898), pp.157–90.

Caputo, J. D. *More Radical Hermeneutics: On Not Knowing Who We Are* (Bloomington: Indiana University Press, 2000).

Caputo, J. D. *On Religion*, 2nd edn (Abingdon, Oxon: Routledge, 2019). https://doi.org/10.4324/9781315197807

Carlyle, T. "Review of John Gibson Lockhart, *Memoirs of the Life of Sir Walter Scott*," *The London and Westminster Review* (January 1838), 154–82.

de Beauvoir, S. *The Ethics of Ambiguity*, trans. B. Frechtman (New York: The Citadel Press, 1970).

de Beauvoir, S. *She Came to Stay*, trans. Y. Moyse and R. Senhouse (London: Harper Perennial, 2006).

Gorner, P. *Heidegger's 'Being and Time': An Introduction* (Cambridge: Cambridge University Press, 2007). https://doi.org/10.1017/cbo9780511808036

Hazleton, L. *Agnostic: A Spirited Manifesto* (New York: Riverhead Books, 2016).

Heidegger, M. *Being and Time*, trans. J. Macquarrie and E. Robinson (Malden, MA: Blackwell Publishing, 1962).

Heidegger, M. *Introduction to Metaphysics*, trans. G. Field and R. Polt (New Haven, CT: Yale University Press, 2000).

Jabès, E. *The Book of Questions, volume 1*, trans. R. Waldrop (Hanover, NH: Wesleyan University Press, 1991).

Jones, H. *The Immortality of the Soul in the Poems of Tennyson and Browning* (London: Philip Green, 1905).

Leivaditis, T. *The Blind Man with the Lamp*, trans. N. N. Trakakis (Limni, Evia: Denise Harvey, 2014).

Leivaditis, T. *Poetry, vol. 1: 1950–1966* [in Greek] (Athens: Metronomos, 2015).

Leivaditis, T. *Violets for a Season*, trans. N. N. Trakakis (Northfield, MN: Red Dragonfly Press, 2017).

McGrath, S. J. *The Early Heidegger and Medieval Philosophy: Phenomenology for the Godforsaken* (Washington, DC: The Catholic University of America Press, 2006). https://doi.org/10.2307/j.ctt2853gt

Moi, T. *Simone de Beauvoir: The Making of an Intellectual Woman* (Oxford: Blackwell, 1994).

Potter, D. *Seeing the Blossom: Two Interviews, a Lecture and a Story* (London: Faber and Faber, 1994).

Russell, B. "A Free Man's Worship," in *Mysticism and Logic and Other Essays* (London: Unwin Books, 1970), pp.40–7.

Scheu, A. K. "The Viability of the Philosophical Novel: The Case of Simone de Beauvoir's *She Came to Stay*," *Hypatia, 27* (2012), 791–809. https://doi.org/10.1111/j.1527-2001.2011.01199.x

Trakakis, N. N. "Postmodern Approaches to Religion," in G. Oppy (ed.), *The Routledge Handbook of Contemporary Philosophy of Religion* (London: Routledge, 2015), pp.32–50.

Trakakis, N. N. "Philosophy and Religious Commitment," *Sophia, 56* (2017), 605–30. https://doi.org/10.1007/s11841-017-0575-z

Trakakis, N. N. "How To Be An Agnostic," *European Journal for Philosophy of Religion, 13* (2021), 179–94. https://doi.org/10.24204/ejpr.2021.3689

Wicks, R. Modern French Philosophy: *From Existentialism to Postmodernism* (Oxford: Oneworld, 2003).

Index

Note: Page numbers followed by "n" denote endnotes.